CULTURES OF

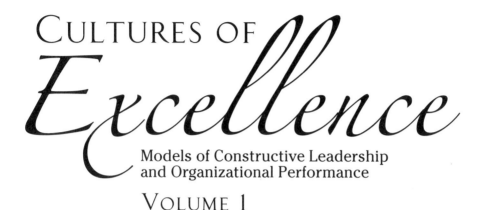

Excellence

Models of Constructive Leadership and Organizational Performance

VOLUME 1

Edited by
Lou Tice, M.Ed. and Glenn Terrell, Ph.D.

©2005 The Pacific Institute®, Inc.

Pacific Institute Publishing
1709 Harbor Avenue SW, Seattle, WA 98126-2049
(206) 628-4800 • www.thepacificinstitute.com
Editorial: Christy A. Watson
Design/Production: Courtney Cook Hopp
Printed in Canada by Friesens Corp.

ISBN 1-930622-04-X

TABLE OF CONTENTS

About the Editors VI
Lou Tice, M.Ed. and Glenn Terrell, Ph.D.

Preface X
Lou Tice, M.Ed., Chairman, The Pacific Institute®, Inc.

PART I

INTRODUCTION
Culture and Organizational Performance 1
Lou Tice, M.Ed. and Glenn Terrell, Ph.D., The Pacific Institute, Inc.
  ♦ Evolution of the Concept of Culture
  ♦ The Pacific Institute's Definition of Culture
  ♦ Organizational Efficacy and Culture
  ♦ Positive Deviance
  ♦ Resilience
  ♦ Upward Spiral
  ♦ Measuring the Culture of Organizations
Chapter Summaries 25
Conclusions 33

PART II

CULTURES OF EXCELLENCE
The Power of the Arrow 35
Brian Wegerle, Managing Director, TPI South Africa

Resolutions for Profitability 53
Joe Atteridge, Managing Partner, Inside Results, LLC

Progress, Not Perfection 71
Co-operative Trust Company of Canada (CTCC)
(now Concentra Financial)
Myrna Bentley, CEO

**The Boddie-Noell Enterprise Experience
with The Pacific Institute** 89
Mike Boddie, CEO of the Hardee's Division of Boddie-Noell Enterprises

**The Winning Culture in Athletics
University of Southern California:
National Collegiate Football Champions, 2003 & 2004** 103
Pete Carroll, Head Football Coach

Culture? In a Car Dealership? You Gotta Be Kidding Me! 111
Mark Leggio, CEO, Mark-Christopher Chevrolet

Modern Terminals—A Company in Transition 121
John Yuen-Chueng Lee, Managing Director

**Transforming From the Inside Out:
Connecticut Light and Power's Course in Excellence** 137
*Lee Olivier, President and Chief Operating Officer of CL&P
Terry Lombardi and David Radanovich*

**Creating a Thriving Culture:
Setting The Pace in Performance** 161
David A. Sabey, CEO, Sabey Corporation

Caterpillar: Employee Engagement and Satisfaction 171
Ernest Skipper, Caterpillar Logistics (USA and UK)

Teacher and Principal Self-Efficacy Studies 183
Jeffrey J. Smith, Ed.D., Roger Freeman, Ed.D., and Theresa Cole, M.Ed.

Hospital Culture – Noble Goals 195
Ken Smithmier, CEO, Decatur Memorial Hospital

Bibliography 207

Acknowledgements

We extend our thanks to the following friends and colleagues for their assistance in the writing and publication of this book, *Cultures of Excellence:*

Diane Tice, for her constant support and creative help in all aspects of the production of the manuscript.

Christy Watson, for her assistance with the follow-up relationships with our client-authors, and her invaluable assistance in editing and proofreading the manuscript.

Courtney Cook Hopp, for her creative design skills and talents, evident on every page of this book.

Ron Schau, for his extraordinary competence in computer skills, so important in the protection of the manuscript.

Jack Fitterer, for providing necessary staff support and for his helpful content suggestions.

Ron Medved for his encouragement and suggestions for the title of the book.

And to everyone else at The Pacific Institute for moral support and, in some instances, specific supportive acts.

We are especially moved by our client-authors' strong, supportive testimonials of the value they received from their work with The Pacific Institute in transforming the cultures of their organizations. A warm "Thank You" from all of us at The Pacific Institute.

About the Editors

Lou Tice, Chairman and Co-Founder of The Pacific Institute, is an internationally recognized authority in the application of research in the cognitive sciences to the challenges facing individuals and organizations today. Translating the research of such notables in the field of psychology as Dr. Albert Bandura of Stanford University, Dr. Martin Seligman of the University of Pennsylvania, and Dr. Gary Latham of the University of Toronto, Lou has provided an education and implementation process that crosses boundaries between individuals, teams, organizations and nations – creating positive, constructive cultures and peak performance.

Author, lecturer and master educator, Lou has a Masters in Education with a focus in the mental health sciences from the University of Washington. In 1971, he and Diane, his wife, founded The Pacific Institute as "a corporation dedicated to human fulfillment." Since then, the Institute has earned an enviable reputation working with Fortune 500 companies, school districts, government agencies, small and medium-sized businesses, the military and countless individuals all over the world. Lou's books include *Smart Talk for Achieving Your Potential* and *Personal Coaching for Results.* 2005 will see the publication of *Leadership is a Performance Art* with USC Football Coach Pete Carroll.

Glenn Terrell, Ph.D. acts as Academic Advisor to The Pacific Institute, coming to the Institute after an 18-year tenure as President of Washington State University. Dr. Terrell earned his B.A. in Political

Science from Davidson College, his M.S. in Psychology from Florida State University, and his Ph.D. from the University of Iowa. Among his numerous honorary degrees and awards are a listing in *Who's Who in America: American Men of Science,* as well as Distinguished Alumnus and Distinguished Graduate of the Department of Psychology from the University of Iowa.

Dr. Terrell has served as President of the National Association of State Universities and Land Grant Colleges; Commissioner for the State of Washington on the Western Interstate Commission for Higher Education; served on the Board of GTE Northwest and West for 23 years; is a member of the Society for Research in Child Development and a Fellow for the American Psychological Association, as well as the American Association for the Advancement of Science. He is the author of numerous articles for professional and academic publications, including *The LETTER* published quarterly by The Pacific Institute. He is also the author of *The Ministry of Leadership: Heart and Theory.*

PREFACE

First and foremost, this is a book about results – proof that the information and education of The Pacific Institute helps individuals and organizations create their own cultures of excellence.

We start with the scholarly literature, research and observations – particularly studies generated by Professor Albert Bandura's Social Cognitive Efficacy Theory. Then, we apply these findings in our client organizations, which trigger tremendous individual and organizational performance.

It is important that you first understand the scientific foundations of the Institute's education, and I have charged Dr. Glenn Terrell – human development psychologist, past President of Washington State University, past president of the National Association of State Universities and Land Grant Colleges, and academic advisor to The Pacific Institute – with this vital piece. He has presented the scope and breadth of history and research in great detail, giving you a broad foundation upon which our client authors/contributors build a remarkable edifice of organizational excellence.

In each and every case, you will see the dramatic results of transforming cultures from the inside out, unleashing the power of the human mind to perform at its highest levels. These are stories of personal and professional triumph, teamwork and organizational excellence. I am proud to have been able to play a part in them.

— *Lou Tice*

PART I

Introduction
CULTURE AND ORGANIZATIONAL PERFORMANCE

By Lou Tice, M.Ed. and Glenn Terrell, Ph.D.

This book speaks to the profound importance of culture in successful organizational development and performance, as viewed by clients of The Pacific Institute. Part I will give you an overview of the concept of culture, as viewed through the eyes of psychologists and researchers over the last half century. In Part II, our clients tell their stories, most of which are based on presentations made at The Pacific Institute's annual Global Conferences, in Seattle, in September 2003 and August 2004. The authors stress the importance of The Pacific Institute's programs in helping them bring about the necessary changes in the cultures of their organizations enabling them to enhance individual and organizational performance.

OUR INTRODUCTION OF THE BOOK CONSISTS OF SIX PARTS:

1. The evolution of the concept of culture

2. The Pacific Institute's concept of organizational culture

3. The enormous impact of Professor Albert Bandura's Efficacy Theory on individual and collective performance, and recent

research stimulated by professor Martin Seligman's Positive Psychology concept, with special reference to the concept of Positive Deviance.

4.   Measuring organizational culture

5.   Brief summaries of the clients' chapters

6.   Conclusions

THE EVOLUTION OF THE CONCEPT OF CULTURE

Margaret Mead's name and research on the cultures of Samoa, New Guinea and Bali, as well as North America, are indelibly imprinted in the American psyche. Mead is perhaps best known for her best-selling *Coming of Age in Samoa.* In this book, she describes the society of Samoa, a project she completed in partial fulfillment of the requirements for her PhD degree from Columbia University. The lasting importance of her work may be best supported by two fac-tors: a) *Coming of Age in Samoa* was, and still is, a best seller, many years after its original publication; and b) Her accomplishments are prominently displayed in the distinguished American Museum of Natural History's Hall of Pacific Peoples. Professor Mead herself has said that, "I have spent most of my life studying the lives of other peoples – faraway peoples – so that Americans might better under-stand themselves." (This information we obtained from Mead's web site.) Professor Mead's work, along with the research of other early scholars seems to suggest that, whether they intended it or not, the concepts of society and culture are interchangeable. For our purpos-es, however, the terms are not interchangeable. Research on societ-ies is a broader undertaking than the focus of attention on culture.

From our perspective, research on societies includes, among other areas, the educational, political, governmental, and human socializa-tion practices of nations, while research on cultures today is more often directed toward the analysis of core values, beliefs and attitudes of all types of organizations within a nation or society. These include, among other entities, businesses, schools, health care organizations, the military, federal and state agencies, automobile agencies, utilities and power companies, sports teams, and financial institutions.

As a matter of fact, in recent years the culture of NASA, the National Aeronautic and Space Administration, has come into question as a factor in the crash of the Shuttle Columbia. There is some indication (Vaughn, D., see Bibliography) that the disaster may have occurred, in part, as a result of a changed culture at the top from a completely technical culture to a bureaucratically controlled business culture, possibly resulting in the erosion of a safety-first engineering culture. A recent article in The Seattle Times by Keith Darce of Newhouse News Service gives evidence that the culture of NASA has changed in some ways and not in others. Steps have been taken to develop a better understanding of the necessity of the managers and the engineers functioning as a team, not ruled by a top down hierarchical system as was the case two years ago with matters of safety the responsibility of engineers and managers – not managers alone – in preparation for and during flights of the spaceship. These meetings of engineers and managers are now held at a horseshoe-shaped table that indicates a meeting of a team, not a facility where one person does all the talking. According to Darce, a recent survey of NASA workers conducted by Behavioral Science Technology, the California company hired to help the agency change its culture, found that the culture had improved. However, the survey also revealed that a number of non-management workers still believe that things haven't changed.

Currently, much attention is being given to the cultures of the FBI and the CIA in connection with the 9/11 tragedy. Formerly, the term "culture" probably would not have been used in these discussions. Instead, the debate probably would have centered on a " breakdown in communication" between the FBI and the CIA. Because of the nature of our times, we expect social scientists soon will be more extensively involved in researching the cultures of these agencies, as well as the Department of Homeland Security and others with responsibilities for the protection of the citizens of our nation. As a matter of fact, an important new book has recently been published, *Culture and Competence: Contexts of Life Success,* by Sternberg, R.J. and Grigorenko, E.L., which emphasizes the importance of our being culturally competent in a world that is rapidly becoming increasingly globalized and complex. The value of this book will be emphasized later, in the context of a discussion about the impact of The Pacific Institute's programs in transforming organizational cultures. Mead's longitudinal research is important to us, because she was one of the early scientists who recognized the importance of societal differences in the understanding of the behavior of nations. It must be added, however, that social scientists – including anthropologists, sociologists, psychologists and educators – in relatively recent years have used the term "culture" to denote theory and research on the behavior of all kinds of organizations within a society, simply because the culture of organizations is exceedingly important to organizational performance, the focus of this book.

It is interesting to note that, in 1952, Kroeber and Kluckhohn reported they found approximately 160 definitions of culture in the literature over the previous 50+ years. So, it is not too much of a stretch to say that there are about as many definitions of culture as there have been scientists and educators defining and researching culture. Countless other definitions have been added since 1952. Jahoda reports that, "The debate about what culture may or may not be remains quite active." Also, comparative psychologists Carel Van Schiak et al are now studying the influence of culture on the behavior of primates, chimps and orangutans in Borneo and Sumatra. They found that many behaviors of these primates are found in some groups yet not in others, and that these differences are "a sign that orangutan groups have at least some hallmarks of what in humans is commonly called culture."

Yale University's Robert J. Sternberg, one of America's most distinguished psychologists and the immediate past president of the American Psychological Association, has done extensive research on the relationship between intelligence and culture. His definition of culture is very similar to The Pacific Institute's: "A set of attitudes, values, beliefs and behaviors shared by a group of people, communicated from one generation to the next via language or some other means of communication." Bandura's social cognitive theory has emphasized the importance of cultural context in today's world with the following statement: "The issues of interest center on how national and global forces interact to shape the nature of cultural life."

No discussion of the evolution of the meaning of the concept of culture is complete without a quote from the distinguished culture scholar, Professor Ralph Linton: "Although the term 'culture' has been used for many years to designate the way of life of a particular society, its exact meaning in terms of content is still vague at certain points. Like a number of other concepts employed in the social sciences, culture has been undergoing a process of gradual delimitation through usage. Such a process accords well with the needs of new and rapidly developing sciences and is the only really workable one in the absence of an ultimate authority to which a difference of opinion can be referred. The end of this process is the emergence of a clear-cut concept designated by a single term whose meaning is clear to all workers in the particular field."

THE PACIFIC INSTITUTE'S DEFINITION OF CULTURE

The concept of culture as employed by The Pacific Institute and our clients is operationally defined by responses to questions on a reliable and valid instrument, the *Organizational Culture and Effectiveness Survey (OCES).* Cook, R., and Szumal, J., have determined the reliability and validity of the *OCES.* In addition to the *OCES,* the following comprises The Pacific Institute's working definition of culture. We do include one dictionary definition, from Webster's New World Dictionary Second College Edition: "The ideas, customs, skills, arts of a given people in a given period." To that definition, we add core values, beliefs and attitudes. You will find the following statements about culture helpful to your understanding of the meaning of culture employed throughout this book. These statements have been developed by Lou Tice as a consequence of his close working relationships with our authors, and include concepts in the Institute's curricula that are particularly useful in our efforts to help our clients transform their cultures as a means of increasing organizational performance.

- Culture is an invisible force.

- Culture is an aggregation of behaviors.

- Cultural traits tend to perpetuate themselves.

- Culture creates comfort zones.

- Constructive leadership constantly challenges current beliefs that no longer serve an organization effectively. The belief makes it so. Human beings tend to act in accordance with the "truth" as they believe it to be, even if it is not the truth.

- "Culture change is a top-down project." Lou Tice, 2004, "Leadership and Changing Cultures."

- When the culture of an organization gets fixed, it is very difficult to change, even when it is obvious that change will lead to a more effective organization. It seems that all meaningful and lasting change starts on the inside, in the imagination, and works its way out into reality.

ORGANIZATIONAL EFFICACY AND CULTURE
Contributions of Bandura, Seligman, Cameron, Dutton & Quinn, Frederickson and others

For approximately one hundred years after the discipline of Psychology was established, the major focus of scholars in psychology was on identifying and treating behavioral problems. In more recent years, two distinguished psychologists have changed that emphasis. Professor Albert Bandura of Stanford University has provided the leadership in the development of a powerful Social-Cognitive theory with emphasis on self- and collective-efficacy as a system for maximizing human potential, clearly a focus on the development of human strengths. Bandura's enormous influence on the direction of Psychology as a discipline during the past several decades, and the limitless applications of his powerful theory to the improvement of human performance, has resulted in his being recognized by his peers as being one of the four most distinguished psychologists of the 20th century. In such evaluations, heavy emphasis is given to the frequency and quality of citations of the scholar's publications.

(We remind you that the Bibliography contains references to Bandura's publications and those of other scholars we refer to in this book. We strongly recommend that you acquire his book, *Self-Efficacy: The Exercise of Control.*)

Attention has also been directed to the University of Pennsylvania's Professor Martin Seligman's introduction of the notion of Positive Psychology, which calls for an increased emphasis by psychologists on human strengths. It is important for you to know that The Pacific Institute has relied mainly on Bandura's work for nearly 20 years, and will continue to do so. More recently, we have added the research of a few working in Seligman's framework in the development of a curriculum that has enabled us to assist our clients in their development of more effective cultures within their organizations, which in turn has helped them to increase productivity and improve internal relationships.

We turn our attention now to a recent publication, *Positive Organizational Scholarship (POS),* edited by K.S. Cameron et al, particularly to those parts devoted to how Positive Psychology can contribute to changes in organizational culture. Although we do recommend that you will benefit from all chapters of *Positive Organizational Scholarship,* we shall devote our attention to three categories of outcomes (positive deviance, resilience and upward spiral) and their benefits to organizations whose cultures stress human strengths and potential. We believe that this book reveals important elements of The Pacific Institute's programs that enable us to help our clients develop a culture that leads to higher levels of performance.

POSITIVE DEVIANCE

Deviant, or deviance, are terms historically used to denote those who deviate in a negative way from established social norms. The authors of Chapter 14 of *Positive Organizational Scholarship* have used the term "positive deviance" in reference to the most admirable of organizational attributes. They discuss, in some detail, five essential attributes of positive deviance in organizations:

1. **Meaning** – Deep personal meaning, with strong intrinsic motivation

2. **"Other" focus** – Consistent with the concept of servant leadership

3. **Self-Determination** – Perceived internal locus of control

4. **Personal Efficacy** – A belief that one can set and reach goals

5. **Courage** – A willingness to take risks

A careful examination of these five factors, necessary for successful facilitation of the concept of positive deviance in organizations, comes close to the approach employed by The Pacific Institute in our work with clients in the development of corporate cultures – work that has proven to be successful over the past 30+ years. However, there is an interesting difference. That difference is in the use of the term "positive deviance" as a description of our product. The concept "positive deviance" adds a powerful dimension to the way we perceive our mission and to our individual and collective confidence (efficacy), resulting in the setting of even more lofty individual and corporate goals than in the past. It bears repeating that the way Spreitzer and Sonenshein (the authors of Chapter 14) describe the factors listed above as necessary to facilitating positive deviance, is, in many ways, what we have been teaching for more than 30 years. We conclude this point with a reminder that it matters what labels we give to concepts. We now see our business to be the creation of positively deviant people and organizations, in the Spreitzer and Sonenshein use of that term, the loftiest goal possible.

RESILIENCE

Resilience is defined by K. M. Sutcliffe and T. J. Vogus, in *Positive Organizational Scholarship,* as "the maintenance of positive adjustment under challenging conditions." Sutcliffe and Vogus further state that, "The domain of resilience is worthy of scholarly attention as it can provide insight into the etiology and course of positive adjustment or adaptability under challenging conditions." Organizational resiliency is increased when members of a group believe they have the ability to act. This belief is more likely to be generated in an organization where human capabilities rather than weaknesses are stressed.

Organizational efficacy figures prominently in promoting resilience. It is widely believed that a group's "shared belief in their conjoint capability to organize and execute the course of action required to produce desired levels of attainment can have a very positive effect on performance under adversity." (Bandura, 1998) Again, collective efficacy is more likely to be encouraged by leaders who place a high premium on human strengths.

According to K.M. Sutcliffe and T.J. Vogus (2003), the following factors are necessary for the development of resilience in organizations:

1. Sufficient resources to build and enhance competence.

2. Increase the amount, access to, and quality of human, social, and material resources available to individuals.

3. Increase the effective utilization of existing resources through flexible structure and interaction experiences.

4. Mobilize mastery motivation system to foster growth and efficacy.

5. Develop and maintain conceptual slack.

6. Foster structures that enable individuals to exercise judgment, discretion, and to make and recover from mistakes.

7. Put people in roles where they can experience success.

8. Foster structures that facilitate learning and skill building and reinforce a learning orientation.

9. Leadership that fosters belief in the group's conjoint capabilities.

10. Develop structures that allow flexibility in rearranging and transferring expertise and resources.

11. Enhance capabilities to quickly process feedback.

UPWARD SPIRAL

Frederickson, B.L., the author of Chapter 11 in *Positive Organizational Scholarship,* proposes a "Broaden and Build Theory" of positive emotions. This theory holds that emotions such as joy, happiness and enthusiasm felt by a single member of an organization can favorably affect an entire organization. This is her definition of "upward spiral." Frederickson further states that, "Joy creates the urge to play, to push limits, explore, and to create."

Expanding on Frederickson's theory, Lou Tice offers the following. The upward spiral in an organization is a new way of looking at an old process; a way of making the formerly invisible visible. The upward spiral is the means to unleash and organize latent capacity to the extent to which human possibilities are enabled to produce extraordinary positive outcomes. It is a way organizations can create and sustain competitive advantage by focusing on how positive emotions can transform individuals and organizations and move them in upward spirals to higher levels of performance. Frederickson's Broaden and Build Theory addresses the understructure of the process for unleashing potential in organizations.

MEASURING THE CULTURE OF ORGANIZATIONS

A working knowledge of this part of our book is essential for anyone who wants to understand how we define and measure the concept of "culture." The client chapters of this book clearly indicate that the clients understand the definition and importance of cultural effectiveness to the success of their organization.

SURVEY OF ADAPTIVE AND NON-ADAPTIVE CULTURES

Kotter and Heskett in their analysis of Adaptive and Non-Adaptive cultures over an 11-year period found that Adaptive Cultures were far more productive than Non-Adaptive cultures. Table 1 below contains the percent increases in Revenue, Stock Price and Net Income for adaptive cultures and non-adaptive cultures.

Table 1 Percent Increase Over 11-Year Period		
	Adaptive (Constructive) Cultures	Non-Adaptive (Defensive) Cultures
Revenue	682%	166%
Stock Price	901%	74%
Net Income	756%	1%

Adaptive Cultures significantly outperformed Non-Adaptive Cultures on all three measures. You will note that in Table 1, the terms Constructive and Defensive are included in parentheses, indicating that Adaptive Cultures in Kotter and Heskett's survey are very similar in definition to Constructive Cultures in the survey used by The Pacific Institute, the *Organizational Culture and Effectiveness Survey (OCES)*. Non-Adaptive Cultures in Kotter and Heskett's study are very similar to Defensive Cultures as defined in the *OCES*. The results of the Kotter and Heskett research were reported by the authors in their book published about ten years ago, and frequently referred to in the research literature on organizational culture.

THE ORGANIZATIONAL CULTURE AND EFFECTIVENESS SURVEY (OCES)

As indicated earlier, The Pacific Institute uses the *Organizational Culture and Effectiveness Survey,* developed by Human Synergistics International, with many client groups to define and measure the effectiveness of *Investment in Excellence®, Imagine 21™,* and other programs used in the client relationship. The *OCES* yields four measures: Organizational Culture, Organizational Effectiveness, Leadership Effectiveness and Personal Effectiveness. Together, these four measures provide a model for measuring the impact of *Investment in Excellence (IIE)* and *Imagine 21 (I-21)* on the culture of client organizations. The high reliability and validity of the *OCES* has been determined as reported in an article by Cook and Szumal.

The Pacific Institute's curricula assist the clients in making the culture of their organizations more conducive to organizational effectiveness. The culture is partially determined by both Leadership and Personal Effectiveness, which the curriculum addresses directly. Therefore, to improve the organization, the culture must be improved; and to improve the culture, Personal and Leadership Effectiveness must be improved. Figure 1 below portrays the four basic components of the model. (We recognize the contribution of Bob Nelson in assisting in the development of this model, and for his joint authorship of the Summer 1998 issue of *The Letter.* This in-

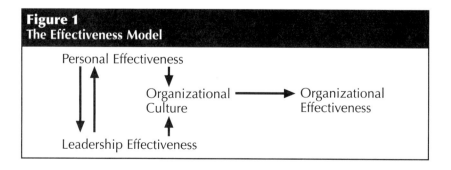

Figure 1
The Effectiveness Model

house quarterly publication contains a thorough discussion of our experience in the use of the *OCES* with many of our clients.)

The *OCES* provides measures of the components in Figure 1. Organizational culture is measured in terms of 12 specific types of behavioral norms. Behavioral norms describe the behaviors that all members of the organization understand are expected of them if they are to fit in and be successful within their organization. As a component of organizational culture, behavioral norms are shaped by the commonly shared assumptions, beliefs, and values of the organization's members and lead to the general patterns of work-related behaviors and attitudes that may be observed. Identifying the norms that guide members' behavior can help us understand the differences that underlie effective versus ineffective organizations. Combining the individual member responses to the *OCES* provides a profile of the shared behavioral expectations that operate within the organization. This profile allows one to determine the strength of the organization's culture. A strong culture is one in which all members agree that a specific set of behaviors are expected. A weak culture is reflected in little agreement between members regarding expectations and/or the lack of a clear set of behavioral norms.

ORGANIZATIONAL EFFECTIVENESS
The *OCES* measures Organizational Effectiveness with four specific factors that influence or shape organizational culture and the outcomes that result: teamwork, role clarity, downward communication, and upward communication.

LEADERSHIP EFFECTIVENESS
Leadership Effectiveness measures and provides feedback to leaders on their impact on others in the organization, as well as strategies and techniques that account for their impact. The five areas of Leadership Effectiveness focus on task emphasis, excellence, consideration, goal definition and communication.

PERSONAL EFFECTIVENESS

Personal Effectiveness measures individual attributes of locus of control, trust, directedness and future outlook. The use of *OCES* allows The Pacific Institute and their clients to quantify organizational culture, develop the strategies and tactics necessary to change the culture as needed, and to monitor the process of change.

The 12 behavioral styles measured by *OCES* are grouped into three major categories: *Passive-Defensive* (consisting of people and security-oriented styles); *Aggressive-Defensive* (consisting of task and security-oriented styles); and *Constructive* (consisting of satisfaction-oriented styles which balance people and tasks).

Each of the three major categories is defined by four cultural styles. The *Passive-Defensive* category consists of Avoidance, Dependent, Conventional and Approval styles; the *Aggressive-Defensive* style includes Oppositional, Power, Competitive, and Perfectionist styles; and the *Constructive* category consists of Achievement, Self-Actualizing, Humanistic-Encouraging and Affiliative styles.

RESULTS

Correlations between Organizational Effectiveness and Culture, Personal Effectiveness and Leadership Effectiveness are .5614, .3077 and .6024 respectively. It follows that:

a) Leadership Effectiveness is more important in determining Organizational Effectiveness than Personal Effectiveness.

b) Culture contributes 31.5% of the factors that account for differences in the effectiveness of organizations.

c) Leadership variables contribute 36.3% of the variability in Organizational Effectiveness; and

d) Differences in Personal Effectiveness contribute only 9.5% of the effectiveness of organizations.

The differences in a and b above are significant at the .01% level of confidence, which means that there is only one chance in a hundred that the differences this great were caused by chance alone. It is surprising that Personal Effectiveness did not appear to be as significant a factor as one would think. We believe that further research with a larger group of clients, and pre- and post-tests will show that Personal Effectiveness is of significant importance in achieving Organizational Effectiveness.

THE EFFECTIVENESS OF OCES IN IDENTIFYING VARIABLES THAT CONTRIBUTE TO ORGANIZATIONAL EFFECTIVENESS

For this purpose, we use the information contained in the circumplexes in Figures 2 through 11 on the following pages.

These figures contain responses of the participants from 28 client organizations. The responses are grouped into the three major categories:

- *Passive-Defensive* (consisting of people and security-oriented styles)

- *Aggressive–Defensive* (task and security styles)

- *Constructive* (satisfaction styles that balance people and tasks)

The total Current Reality responses (1083), and Vision responses (261) of our 28 client groups are pictured in Figures 2 and 3 respectively. The Current Reality profile is slightly more Defensive than Constructive, while the profile for Vision is strikingly more Constructive than Defensive.

- On the *Constructive Defensive* dimension, the upper 25% saw their organization as the most constructive, while the lower 25% saw their organization as most defensive. (See Figures 4 and 5)

- On *Organizational Effectiveness,* the profiles of those who saw their organization as most effective saw their organization as being strikingly more constructive while those who saw their organization as least effective saw their organization as more defensive. (See Figures 6 and 7)

- On *Leadership Effectiveness,* Figures 8 and 9 indicate clearly that effective leaders are associated with constructive styles while ineffective leaders are associated with defensive cultures.

- Figures 10 and 11 reveal less distinct differences for *Personal Effectiveness* between the cultures of those who described themselves as most effective compared to those who saw themselves as least effective. Predictably, the former group saw their culture as more constructive, while the latter saw their organizational culture as less effective.

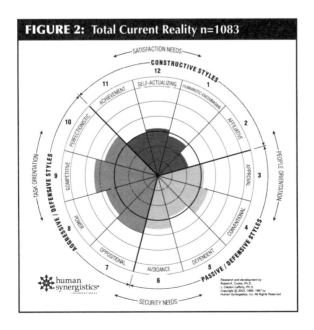

FIGURE 2: Total Current Reality n=1083

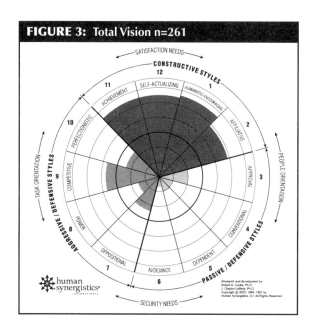

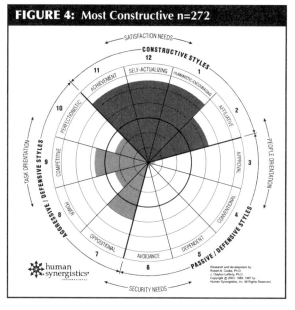

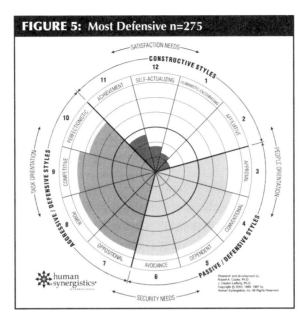

FIGURE 5: Most Defensive n=275

FIGURE 6: Most Effective Organizations n=273

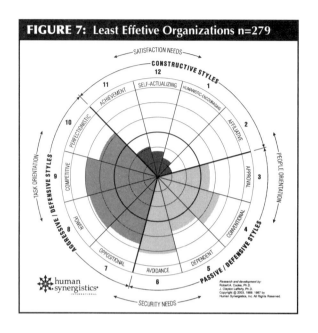

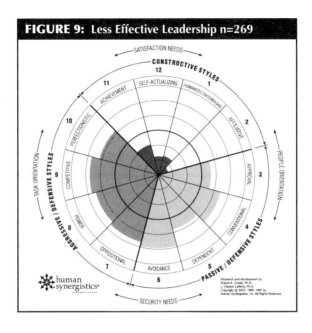

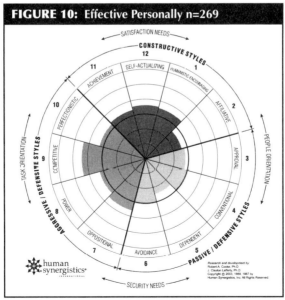

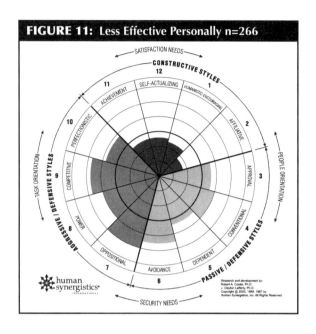

FIGURE 11: Less Effective Personally n=266

Chapter Summaries

Thus far, we have dwelled on the important changes in the meaning and the measurement of "culture." We have given special attention to The Pacific Institute's meaning of the term, as developed by Lou and our clients; and the importance of another measurement instrument of culture *(OCES)* as an operational definition of the term.

We now come to the main thrust of the book, the opinions of our clients about the effectiveness of The Pacific Institute in helping them to experience success by creating excellence in their organizational culture, resulting in an unprecedented high level of performance. It is customary for editors of books to provide an overview of the contents of the book. Significantly, you will notice that we are presenting a wide variety of client stories, proving once again that the education offered by The Pacific Institute transcends categories of organizations. Represented here are large and small organizations; leadership in sports, healthcare, nuclear power, finance and sales; as well as public education. These reports cross international borders, confirming that culture and leadership issues are people issues, and performance – high performance – is the ultimate goal.

THE POWER OF THE ARROW
Brian Wegerle, Managing Director, TPI South Africa

In an interesting analysis of how to build an effective culture,
Wegerle uses the metaphor of an arrow to develop his concept of a
thriving culture. He begins with the assumption that the culture of
all organizations consists of the individual, which he refers to as the
"Me"; the department or division as the "We"; and the whole organization as the "Us." The challenge to leaders, in Wegerle's analysis,
is to create an organization that recognizes and rewards the values,
strengths and contributions of individuals (the Me's), while at the
same time, building commitment on the part of everyone to the We's
and the Us as an essential requirement of working collaboratively in
the development of an effective culture. The word that best describes these relationships is "alignment." He further states there are
three ingredients of commitment – Able, Allowed, and Willing – and
that "There must be interventions at all three levels in order to create a thriving, or willing, allowed culture."

RESOLUTIONS FOR PROFITABILITY
American Airlines Direct Marketing Corporation
Joe Atteridge, Managing Partner, Inside Results, LLC

When Joe Atteridge took over the reigns of a subsidiary of the AMR
Corporation, the company was losing money. They recognized the
need for a change in the culture, and engaged The Pacific Institute to
assist them in this effort. The Institute's programs proved to be ex-
traordinarily helpful, especially in those areas where the need for a
fresh approach was important for a cultural change. Enthusiasm for
the Institute's centerpiece program, *Investment in Excellence®*, was so
high that it became the company's foundation for all employee training. Teams became more effective, resulting in improved quality.

Moving from AMR, Atteridge invested in REZsolutions, a hotel reservation business that also engaged The Pacific Institute, with similar results. Atteridge reports that REZsolution's business doubled "year after year," and he, in his own words, attributes their success to "information and skills learned in *Investment in Excellence.*"

PROGRESS, NOT PERFECTION
Co-operative Trust Company of Canada (CTCC)
(now Concentra Financial)
Myrna Bentley, CEO

Ms. Bentley became President and CEO of CTCC in 1997 at a very challenging time of rapid change in financial institutions across Canada. Competition was unprecedented, a condition that required fundamental changes in the way business was conducted. A new corporate culture was required. To quote Ms Bentley, at this time, "Enter The Pacific Institute and Lou Tice." The experience with the Institute and Ms. Bentley's leadership skills resulted in the adoption of a leadership style that she defined as "traveling the high road" emphasizing Trust, Compassion, Courage, Honesty, Respect, and Integrity. Ms. Bentley reports dramatic increases in profitability and just as important, increases in employee engagement and pride.

THE BODDIE-NOELL ENTERPRISE EXPERIENCE WITH THE PACIFIC INSTITUTE
Mike Boddie, CEO of the Hardee's Division of Boddie-Noell Enterprises

Boddie-Noell Enterprises ranks among the top five privately held companies in North Carolina and Virginia, and the sixth largest retail food franchisee in the United States in 2003, according to Restaurant Finance Monitor. Mike Boddie became the CEO of the Hardee's Division of Boddie-Noell Enterprises in 1995. In a tremendous undertaking, officers, support staff, district managers, vice-presidents and general managers, among others, attended *Imagine 21™, Pathways to Excellence®,* and *Purpose in Life: Ethics and Organizational Success®.* 49 Facilitators from the home office and District Manager personnel administered these programs to Hardee's region of nine areas, with 39 restaurants in each area. Mike reports that between June 2003 and June 2004 the average unit volume increased $100,000, for total additional sales of $31,700,000 without adding one single restaurant. *"Life is good!"* Mike exclaims.

THE WINNING CULTURE IN ATHLETICS
UNIVERSITY OF SOUTHERN CALIFORNIA: NATIONAL
COLLEGIATE FOOTBALL CHAMPIONS, 2003 & 2004
Pete Carroll, Head Football Coach

Coach Carroll describes the principles he uses in the development of a consistent winning culture at the University of Southern California: Direction (goals), Beliefs, Authenticity, Expectations, Self-Talk, Team Conscience, Thought Control, Visualization and Accountability. These same concepts are central to The Pacific Institute's program's success in assisting client organizations in their development of a sustained culture of optimal performance. Coach Carroll praises Lou's and TPI's development of well-organized programs based on research that supports many of the principles he has been using for some time, and for Lou's valuable specific and general influence that has been beneficial to him in his coaching success.

CULTURE? IN A CAR DEALERSHIP? YOU GOTTA BE KIDDING ME!
Mark Leggio, CEO, Mark-Christopher Chevrolet

Mark Leggio tells an interesting, convincing and sometimes amusing story about his experiences with The Pacific Institute in changing the culture of his automobile dealership. In the first page of his chapter, Mark outlines what he calls the "Key" to the successful implementing of The Pacific Institute's curriculum: "Once you've rolled people through the curriculum, how long does it remain effective? Are your people still working on the assimilation of the skills they learned from TPI? Are they still engaged?" We particularly like his conception of TPI's programs: ". . .The Pacific Institute's information is not a training program. Rather it is a way of life for our organization."

MODERN TERMINALS---A COMPANY IN TRANSITION
John Yuen-Chueng Lee, Managing Director

John Lee reports that in the decade of the 1990's, as Hong Kong became one of the largest gateways into and out of China, Modern Terminals experienced difficult business times. Goals and strategies were developed for the future, with the emphasis on changing the culture of the organization. The Pacific Institute Australasia was engaged to assist Modern Terminals in reaching this important goal. To quote the CEO, "TPI was particularly helpful because of their skill in helping us develop a strong belief that we can accomplish our goals." The results were outstanding: Increases in market share, 8.7%; operational margin, 12%; return on assets, 18%; and return on equity, 17%. Profit after tax increased 47%, while dividends distributed to shareholders increased 120%. At the same time, soft costs decreased 21%; fixed costs decreased 62% and variable costs per container decreased 36%.

TRANSFORMING FROM THE INSIDE OUT: CONNECTICUT LIGHT AND POWER'S COURSE IN EXCELLENCE
Lee Olivier, President and Chief Operating Officer of CL&P
Terry Lombardi and David Radanovich

Lee Olivier, President and Chief Operating Officer of CL&P was appointed in 2001. His charge was to "transform CL&P from a good, traditional electric utility into a top-performing one." His plan was to create a culture with four strategies. Each strategy was consistent not only with his change principles, but also with the philosophical foundation of Lou Tice and The Pacific Institute "utilizing key results areas that drive success as the focus of organizational change." The success of the cultural transformation is best summarized in Lee's own words. "The mindset has changed at CL&P. The people now see the visions of two years ago becoming a reality. The *Imagine 21™* experience provided them the opportunity to see new horizons that many never envisioned as future possibilities."

SETTING THE PACE IN PERFORMANCE
David A. Sabey, CEO, Sabey Corporation

David Sabey writes a convincing story about the influence of Lou and Diane Tice, and the programs of The Pacific Institute, on his personal development and on his many business successes. His reference to The Pacific Institute's product as the "software" of our set of capabilities is fresh and on target. Sabey then describes the benefits of TPI's software in the development of his many numerous business enterprises, including, among many, the million square foot facility for Ebox of the world, which also houses all of MSNBC and half of Hotmail, as well as Nordstrom's Internet. Sabey has been supplier for Wal-Mart and Target. His clients also include Barnes and Noble,

Sun Sportswear, Seattle Post Intelligencer, Department of Social and Health Services, and The Boeing Company.

CATERPILLAR: EMPLOYEE ENGAGEMENT AND SATISFACTION
Ernest Skipper, Caterpillar Logistics (USA and UK)

Ernest Skipper learned the value of The Pacific Institute's program, *Investment in Excellence®* in creating revitalized cultures, and tells this story from the perspectives of his several high-level management positions in the Caterpillar organization. For example, as the leader of the Caterpillar Distribution Services, he established a goal to "drastically reduce costs without reducing service quality." He reports that they exceeded the goal of productivity improvement for 2000 by 148%.

The Bold Goals project was an accelerated program "designed to establish Caterpillar Logistics as the best logistics company – lowest cost, highest quality, best service in the world." Ernest reports excellent results of the Bold Goals project in terms of behavioral and operational criteria. The project raised annual productivity improvement from 3% to 34% over the following three years. He also reports dramatic improvements in behavioral, operational and financial categories.

TEACHER AND PRINCIPAL SELF-EFFICACY STUDIES
Jeffrey J. Smith, Ed.D., Roger Freeman, Ed.D., and Theresa Cole, M.Ed.

This chapter is a review of two recent studies conducted to measure the effectiveness of The Pacific Institute's program *21 Keys for High Performance Teaching and Learning™* on teachers and principals. Jeff Smith, Ed.D. is the Director of Curriculum and Instruction for the

Paradise Valley Unified School District in Phoenix, Arizona. Roger Freeman, Ed.D. served as an elementary school teacher prior to becoming the Director of Assessment for the Paradise Valley Unified School District. Their quantitative results provide strong evidence of the Institute's effectiveness in the field of education

Theresa Cole, M.Ed, is a master educator with over 24 years experience working in the classroom and at all levels of education, as well as being a Project Director for The Pacific Institute. Cole's material provides qualitative results in the form of testimonials.

HOSPITAL CULTURE – NOBLE GOALS
Ken Smithmier, CEO, Decatur Memorial Hospital

Ken Smithmier stresses the importance of knowing who your competition is, and of being motivated by what he labels "Noble Goals" rather than just a desire to win. He agrees that hospitals, like all businesses must compete to survive, but urges that special attention be given by businesses to strive for the accomplishment of personal and corporate goals that in some way elevate the human condition. Ken then uses three true stories to illustrate his points: Smarty Jones's losing performance at the Belmont Stakes to a long-shot horse (after Smarty previously had outrun the two horses who were supposed to be his main competition), to illustrate the idea that we, like horses make the mistake of not having a clear idea of what or who our competition may be; and to further illustrate the value of "Noble Goals," Ken tells the stories of a Quaker, John Woolman, and Eric Clapton.

CONCLUSIONS

The Pacific Institute's application of social-cognitive theory as developed by Albert Bandura, and his students and other devotees of his theory, is an ideal approach to the development of programs that will assist our client organizations in their efforts to attain optimal performance. The main thrust of our approach with clients is to teach them the power of cognitive skills in building individual and collective efficacy, which in turn will provide a sound basis for establishing necessary changes in culture.

We repeat the importance of the concepts of Positive Deviance, resilience, the upward spiral, as well as other ideas expressed by the authors of *Positive Organizational Scholarship* as they are related to human strengths, and their importance to the establishment of a corporate culture that produces happiness, engagement and increased productivity. In fact, as of now, we will use the concept of Positive Deviance as an accurate term to define the essence of what we create at The Pacific Institute.

As Lou Tice puts it, underlying the cognitive process is the power of thinking embodied in the phrase, "We move toward what we think about." Efficacy is a belief that we can set and reach individual and organizational goals of our choice. Our experience has been that if we help our clients develop a high level of efficacy, individual and collective, they will set lofty goals, and be capable of overcoming the resistance of those still functioning under a culture that is no longer compatible with new goals. You will observe that the authors of the chapters of this book express the belief that the two centerpiece programs of The Pacific Institute, *Investment in Excellence*® and *Imagine 21*™, were of significant importance in their efforts to create organizational cultures that enabled them to reach lofty goals.

We mentioned earlier the significance of a recent book authored by Sternberg and Grigorenko, *Culture and Competence.* This book has obvious general significance in the global world of today, where competencies in the establishment of effective relationships throughout the world are essential to the success of nations and organizations. The Pacific Institute teaches a culture-free competence, or efficacy, which helps clients enhance performance. We have reason to believe that those same competencies can be taught to individuals, organizations or nations seeking skills that enable them to enhance their performance in relationships with other societies.

Finally, we express our appreciation to our client-authors for recognizing our ability to be of assistance to them in the development of cultures that enhanced their performance and brought them personal satisfaction.

PART II

THE *Power* OF THE *Arrow*
MOVING FROM ME TO WE TO US

By Brian Wegerle,
Managing Director TPI — South Africa

If I were to summarize what I'm feeling right now, I'd have to say I'm overwhelmed with a feeling of gratitude. I'm grateful to all those from the worldwide Pacific Institute family represented here. I'm not sure that everyone here appreciates what it's like to be from South Africa, where not long ago we had what I would call "polecat" status. We were not a popular nation, especially if you were a white male.

The Pacific Institute (TPI) members have pulled us in, made us feel welcomed, and most important, they have equipped us to be relevant in our little part of the world. I'm really grateful to Lou and Diane, and to every TPI person here. It's great to be connected to a team that lifts us up, and enables us to stand a little higher.

I'm grateful for the TPI curriculum. In my previous career, I worked at the executive or board level of some big companies in South Africa. I attended every course I could, sponsored by major universities and other organizations in the UK and USA. I have known distinguished people like Peter Senge, Pat Mclaggen, and Don Bick. I learned much from these experiences.

But I must say the TPI curriculum is the single most important learning event of my life. More than that, it is a life-long experience. We continue to apply this curriculum to our careers and personal goals.

I'm grateful to my young bride, Jenni, who, when I left the corporate comfort zone and started pounding the pavement establishing The Pacific Institute in South Africa, believed in me and stayed with me. I am also grateful to my colleagues in TPI South Africa, who are here, and the 27 others back home; and to our clients, one of whom is here, Willie Rossouw.

Willie heads up a global process for the SASOL Organization, a company that employs nearly 40,000 people around the world, and has a multi-billion dollar turnover. He has taken over companies here in America, Germany and Italy. His job is to facilitate worldwide what they call the Net Gain Process, a system designed to reduce the total cost of ownership, including the total cost earning and capital assets. He has partnered with us like I cannot believe. He volunteered to participate in the Global Conference. He will tell you that TPI's curriculum has helped him bring back a savings of 1.8 billion Rand. That's about $200 million that has been added to the bottom line through the TPI curriculum. Neil Straker and others may ask how we know that TPI alone is responsible for all of this large increase in savings? Willie would say that it would have taken much longer, if it happened at all, to generate increases this large without TPI's intervention. I salute Willie and all of his people. In South Africa, we have a saying, "Aboontu," meaning, "I cannot be fully me without you." So, together, we are taking on this great challenge that we face.

I'm going to talk about the whole dynamic of the "power of the arrow." (See Figure One) But first, let's think about what has happened today. Lou has spoken convincingly about the importance of culture in organizational change. He has shown us that even one person can help influence a culture. We have heard about a very significant success story of an entrepreneur building a mega business in this country. We've heard about improving performance in schools in an under-privileged area; about Michael O'Brien's ideas about measuring the concept of culture; about a mountaineer climbing Mount Everest. And now, here's this Wegerle dude talking about the Power of the Arrow.

FIGURE 1

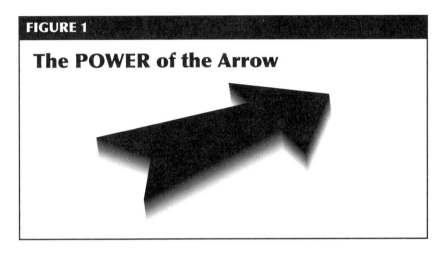

The POWER of the Arrow

I believe it is accurate to say that all of the presentations today have been directed toward the improvement of performance. Is there a set of universal concepts that have been validated empirically and in practice, that when applied to a business, school or other organizations would improve performance? The answer is "Yes." We are hearing at this conference some dramatic, performance improvement experiences with the application of TPI's programs. But there are still improvements that can be made in our continuing effort to reach optimal human performance. The key word in this continuing effort is "optimal." I use the symbol or metaphor, "power of the arrow," to illustrate how we can develop or create a thriving culture in any organization.

The arrow is a metaphor for you and me. It reflects direction, distinctiveness, and in some sense, power. But it also symbolizes the "WIIFM," or "What's in it for me." Let's first elaborate on the distinctiveness of the "me," followed by the development of the importance of the "we" and the "us." All three are important in the development of a thriving culture.

DISTINCTIVENESS

We are all distinctive or unique. There are approximately six billion of us on the planet. I don't know who counted them, but let's assume that the figure six billion is approximately correct. Yet each of us has thumbprints that are absolutely unique.

There is no person who has walked precisely the journey of life, nor has precisely the same degree of efficaciousness that you have. We are so unique, and the more efficacious we are, the more powerful our arrow is, and that is a wonderful thing.

Quoting Robert Fulghum (See Figure Two), "We are as different from one another on the inside of our heads as we appear to be different from one another on the outside of our heads. We are different in terms of what we know, what we think, what we believe, and in our strategies for coping. We're different in our purpose, we're different in our skills, and so all of this difference is resonant with power." To

FIGURE 2

"We are as different from one another on the inside of our heads as we appear to be different from one another on the outside of our heads.

"We are different in terms of what we know, what we think and believe and in our strategies for coping."

— Robert Fulghum

this I add that these differences are desirable and challenging, especially in efficacious people.

For the purpose of building a thriving culture, there is a complicating aspect to the uniqueness of people described above. Let me illustrate. From my TPI office window back home in South Africa, I asked 15 delegates attending one of our programs to look out the window to observe, record, and report what they saw. Guess what? Their reports revealed that the events and objects they saw were exceedingly different. There were 15 different versions of reality. Can you see the subtle implications for this? Even efficacious people (and these people are very efficacious) have the potential for creating clash and fragmentation. Leaders often have the challenge of people wanting to go in different directions. Of course, sometimes we are faced with, for example, a safety issue that Lou referred to earlier, where it may become necessary to enforce a non-smoking rule for those with responsibility for managing the boiler room.

Now we want to build a team of efficacious individuals who want to climb a mountain, while others may have different, but no less important desires like developing a business or a public agency. So, you see the colorful kaleidoscope of the energy building, and in some instances waiting to explode.

Now, refer to Figure Three, the goal. To each arrow, you want to put a word "me." That's me, one arrow, me. We must move now from "me" to "we." To do so, we must harness the differences, and get them to move in a cohesive direction. The challenge, of every leader in this room today, is to harness that energy – to retain the power of me, but not allow the strength of me to overwhelm, compromise or weaken the quality of we. Still, you cannot get a strong we, a strong team, if you don't stimulate the development, the inspiration and direction of each me.

FIGURE 3

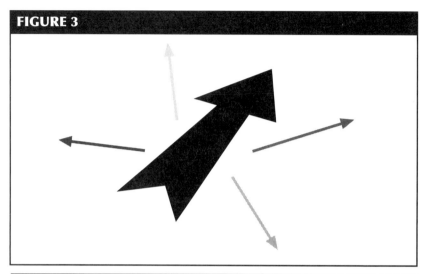

FIGURE 4

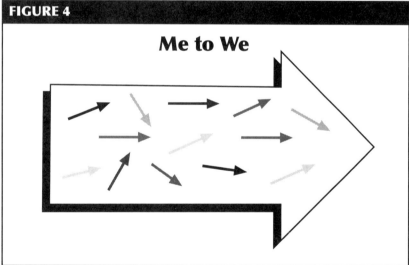

The team is totally dependent on each me, each person, taking his or her place efficaciously and strongly. How do we get this flow? (See Figure Four) You will see inside of that arrow, which is the team or the "we," a multiplicity of different arrows. Those are the "me's" still retaining their uniqueness, and their color, not flying perfectly in the direction of the big arrow, because one needs a bit of "iron sharpening iron." In other words, the "me's" need to spark with one another to insure the desired flow.

But the "we," as healthy as it is, could also cause a problem. In Figure Four, the team arrows are flowing in different directions. In the corporate world, and perhaps in any world, we would call those silos. Silos start forming fragmented groups of people who have aligned themselves cohesively, but they clash with each other. For example, marketing clashing with production, sales people with engineering folk. The power of the arrow is the challenge that we face.

How then, do we build an effective, successful organizational environment where we are culturally different in terms of language, gender, values, hopes, and dreams? Let me redefine that challenge, and then go to the next one.

We want a thriving culture, "me" to "we" to "us," where the different teams are aligned and focused. How do you do that? (See Figures Five and Six) We all want that, but how many of us have it? Every leader of government and corporate organization that I have spoken to says this is their most difficult challenge.

How do we get large, complex organizations with hundreds or thousands of people to develop a thriving culture where individual needs are aligned with the needs of the organization? We all want that, but how many of us actually have it?

An examination of some of the important trends in the workplace may suggest some answers to this critically important question. One trend was discussed in a previous Global Conference several years ago. Lou and Marty Seligman held a stimulating dialogue at the conference. Marty was asked what he had learned about the challenges faced by business organizations at a recent international meeting of psychologists and business leaders. His one sentence response was, "Never before in the developed world have people been so well educated, so wealthy, so technologically advanced, and yet so unhappy."

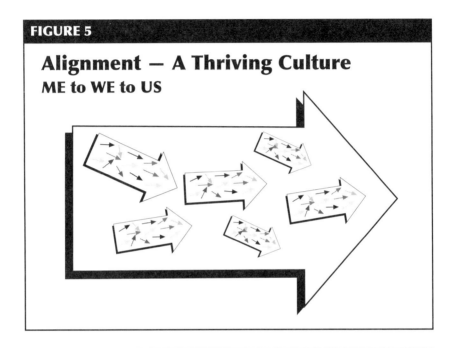

FIGURE 5

Alignment — A Thriving Culture
ME to WE to US

FIGURE 6

The Key Challenges in Transformation

1. How do you get large, complex organizations with multiple hundreds and even thousands of people to move from "here" to "there"?

2. How do you, in this large organization, get the individual members' needs aligned with the needs of the organization?

3. How do you get people with different backgrounds, agendas, dreams, skills and purposes to harmonize and happily "sing off the same song sheet"?

Another important related trend is the increasing number of people whose greatest goal at work is to stop work. I don't know whether or not this is true in other nations represented here. Our work in South Africa suggests that this seems to be a disturbing trend. I'm finding more and more people dreaming of early retirement when they can do what they want to do! Can you imagine the implications of these trends on our ability to build an engaged, committed and aligned culture in our organizations? Think of the implications of these trends on performance! We must be realistic about these trends. It would not surprise me if some of us attending this conference were goal-setting to stop work.

One final quote of the International Chairman of Deloitte, addressing the problem mentioned by Seligman: "We're making our organizations more efficient and more productive with high levels of quality and vastly improved performance, but our people are getting sicker." Also, we often hear the platitudes of many corporate leaders stressing the goal of becoming world class. Our dilemma here is how on earth are we going to build a world class anything with people who can't wait to stop doing what they're doing? These conditions are real, and we must deal with them to realize our goal of building optimally performing cultures.

Some would say I should not be dwelling on the negative. I am only being realistic. These are trends that must be dealt with as we pursue our goal of building high quality organizations where people are performing at the limits of their capability.

Earlier in the day, it was mentioned that many management consultants have concluded that the majority of transformation initiatives fail. Someone asked about how we get leaders to take the initiatives beyond being just another program, or programs, and in doing so, we develop the BOHICA Syndrome. "BOHICA" is an acronym for

"Bend over, here it comes again." And if you stay down long enough, when you come up, maybe the previous program is gone, and a new program is upon us. In fact, this is a trend that we're starting to see emerging more and more in the workplace. The fact is that it has a very negative effect on commitment in the workplace.

All of this ties back to culture, the power of the arrow, the power of culture. A culture by definition involves me, we and us. (See Figure Five) Now, can we find a carefully designed organizational process that enables each one of the three levels – me, we, and us – to experience the quality of thriving?

The CEO of a big chemical company in Germany, Robert Powell, puts it this way: "I can say, from my vantage point, that more good business strategies have been destroyed by incomparable corporate structures than by anything else. It is much easier to change the strategy than to change the culture."

Why is it that we see so many cultural change programs, and yet nothing seems to change? How then can we approach this differently? At TPI we are experiencing some success in understanding the dynamics of cultural change and its effect on organizational performance.

FIGURE 7

A Thriving Culture Making the Extra-Ordinary Ordinary
The disciplines and key concepts required to do this in a structured way.

"A gentle, kind, but determined persistence."
– Lou Tice

A thriving culture may be described as making the extraordinary ordinary. (See Figures Five, Six and Seven, especially Figure Seven) You will find that there are processes and disciplines of diligence, that when one applies these disciplines and key concepts in a structured way, you find a breakout possibility of serious note. To quote a famous gentleman: "A gentle, kind, but determined persistence."

I heard Lou say that we need a long obedience in the same direction to bring about change, and we also need to embrace knowledge that has been scientifically tested and practiced in the workplace. After implementing these initiatives with our clients, we find the fruit of change, where the culture dramatically breaks out into new levels of high performance.

The key word in this process is commitment, which means giving my everything, my best effort in the pursuit of organizational goals. (Figures Seven and Eight indicate the three ingredients of commitment: Able, Allowed, and Willing.)

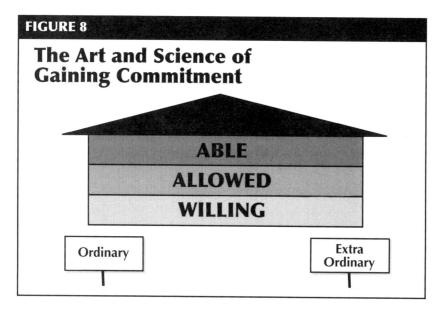

FIGURE 8

The Art and Science of Gaining Commitment

ABLE

ALLOWED

WILLING

Ordinary

Extra Ordinary

My own research on culture is starting to show that if you are able, allowed and willing, you have commitment. Let's start first at the personal level, the "me" level. If I feel willing, which is an internal concept; if I feel allowed, which is both an environmental and inside concept; and, if I feel able, the ingredients of commitment are present. If you don't have all three of these ingredients, you don't have a thriving culture; you don't have what we call a UeVP, which is the ability to perform in a value added way. People may have competence, knowledge, may even have skill and understanding. They may even be willing, but in South Africa, they weren't allowed. Not being allowed implodes the possibility of optimal performance. Likewise, you can find people who are able, who are allowed, but for some reason, they aren't willing. You aren't going to find the required energy that Dave Sabey mentioned.

Now, the willing, allowed and able dimensions must occur at three levels: the "me," the "we" (the team, department or division) and the "us" (the whole organization). There must be interventions at all three levels in order to create a thriving, or willing, allowed and able culture.

With a metaphor of ecology, see Figure Nine. You will see a plant or a potting process at the "me" level. That plant may be in a nursery where it's being nurtured for growth. A plant on its own can be very attractive, but its purpose is obscure. A plant needs to migrate and move into and amongst other plants.

The metaphor, gardening, pertains to the disciplines necessary in order to bring the best of the "me" into a healthy "we." But gardens do not always occupy our thoughts and actions. Many of us would be busy with our businesses, schools, or government departments, sectors, or divisions. The principle is the same.

If you are thriving at the "we" level, at the garden level, it's not enough if the total organization isn't developing some health, some structure.

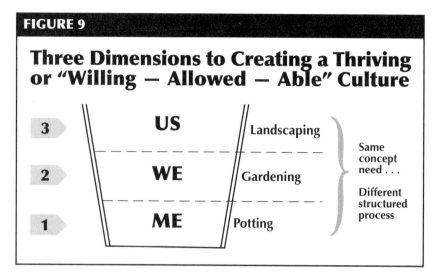

FIGURE 9

Three Dimensions to Creating a Thriving or "Willing — Allowed — Able" Culture

Many gardens together we would call landscaping, or the "us."

Again, referring to Figure Nine, you cannot attend to one of the three dimensions, Willing, Allowed, and Able at the expense of the others. For example, you cannot do just team-building and think you're going to change your organization. If team-building is your only intervention, you are likely to elicit a "So what?" response. By the same token, if an organization only conducts a cultural values survey, any "us" type of intervention, the same "So what?" response will follow.

It follows that one needs carefully planned and designed interventions at all three levels. Continuing the plant metaphor, a plant would need water, sun, soil and air in order to thrive. Gardens and landscapes need the same conditions. Methods of providing these needs would, of course, differ. For the plant, a watering container; for the garden, one would need a hose; and for the landscape, perhaps an irrigation system.

The Pacific Institute's curriculum is equally applicable to the "me," "we," and "us" levels, in creating a thriving Willing, Allowed and Able

Culture. We in South Africa are using *Investment in Excellence*® to improve the performance of "me." We also have another application of the same curriculum that improves the strength of both "we" and "us." Together around the world we're collaborating at bringing the best practices of all our offices together so that everybody may enjoy the benefits and processes we all have found both helpful and effective.

I do know that TPI people at the offices in UK and others are busy helping develop the three dimensional framework presented here. I am convinced that one of the disciplines in the whole process of breaking through from "me" to "we" to "us" is what I label a Strategic Commitment-Gaining Process appearing in Figure Ten. This process will help you to understand how one goes through the personal, team and group levels.

Willie and his team have had much experience working with the Strategic Commitment-Gaining Process in the development of effective cul-

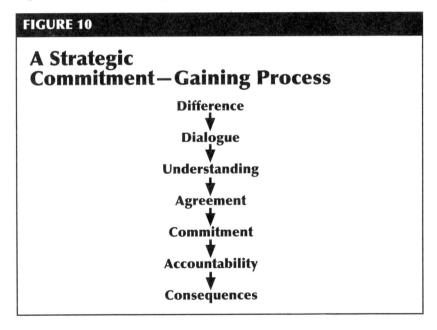

FIGURE 10

A Strategic Commitment—Gaining Process

Difference
↓
Dialogue
↓
Understanding
↓
Agreement
↓
Commitment
↓
Accountability
↓
Consequences

tures. For this reason, he was asked to work with this process in different countries where he had businesses, for example Italy, Germany, USA. Because of the language differences, the only folk who could help them break through across the countries and language groups were the folk who were schooled in this discipline. Referring again to Figure Ten, one moves from differences to dialogue. Metaphorically, dialogue is iron-sharpening, challenge to challenge, people coming together and declaring their differences, describing their different world views, and through that dialogue understanding emerges.

And yet, understanding is not powerful enough. Understanding won't necessarily bring us together. But, where there is agreement, there is power. Once we agree, there is commitment. When there is commitment, you can hold people accountable. You can hold people accountable if there are consequences. TPI very carefully processes people from "me" to the "we" and "us."

Figure Eleven illustrates the movement of the group from "me" to "we." The dimensions (concepts) in the TPI education establish the creative tension, current reality, and a picture of a much better future. Then the fourth little box, the how, is invented along the way. These are process disciplines that you are familiar with, but when done in teams, it's quite powerful.

Figure Twelve, again metaphorically conveys the team concept. The little dots on the tree represent the team concept. Where would you say the most senior team is in Figure Twelve? Typically, we would say at the top of the tree. Not in this instance. The top team is sitting where the power switch is, where the electric current comes from the wall. They generate the legitimacy, the process dynamic, the energy and power throughout the whole organization until every light comes on. The light shining on the whole tree is our entire organization, aligned to achieve the goals of the entire group.

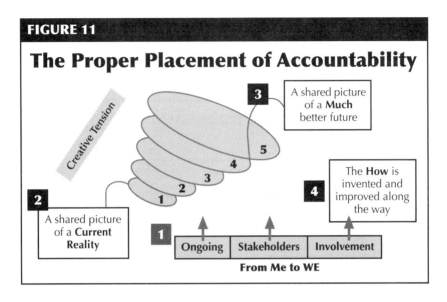

FIGURE 11

The Proper Placement of Accountability

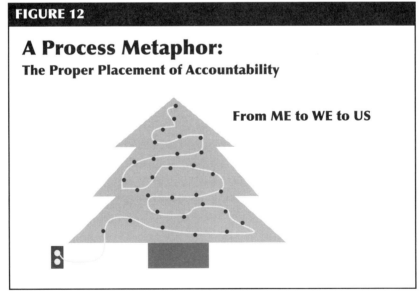

FIGURE 12

A Process Metaphor:
The Proper Placement of Accountability

From ME to WE to US

There is much detail inside of all of this process dynamic. It takes a structured process at all three levels to bring it about. When it comes, it is powerful enough for these things to add lots of economic value to your enterprises. It also leads to dramatically transformed communities and schools, as we have experienced at CENEX – hopefully, some day, to transformed nations.

In closing, I address TPI people in this room, TPI staff, clients and others with this affirmation: "We are pulling together with our strong collective belief, experiencing levels of breakout that have never been seen or dreamed of before."

Resolutions FOR PROFITABILITY
AMERICAN AIRLINES DIRECT
MARKETING CORPORATION

By Joe Atteridge, Managing Partner, Inside Results, LLC

I thought I would tie together a lot of the concepts we've heard the last couple of days, and share that in the light of my own success, using The Pacific Institute's (TPI) curriculum over the past fifteen years. Actually, I used the program three separate times in three different organizations. I'm going to talk about our experience in two of those organizations, including the critically important lessons we learned about how to implement the curriculum.

First of all, I think it would be helpful for you to have an idea of the challenge. I was interviewing for a job with a subsidiary of the AMR Corporation, the parent of American Airlines. They were describing to me what my responsibilities would be. They used words like "challenge" and "opportunity" that I'm sure we all have heard, maybe in interviews, or in discussions among each other. When I accepted their offer, I found "current reality" meant revenue was shrinking. In fact, it had dropped fifty percent in the last year and the subsidary was unprofitable. It had an eleven million dollar loss, and ninety percent of the sales came from one client. (See Table One)

TABLE 1

The Challenge at American - 1987

- **American Airlines Direct Marketing Corporation (AADMC)**
  - **"Challenges"**
    - Sales dropped 50% in past year and profits had evaporated to $11 million loss
    - 90% of revenue from one client
  - **"Leadership"**
    - No vision or strategy
    - Highly fractured team (AA and non-AA)
    - Employee turnover over 200%
  - **"State-of-the-art facilities in solid industry"**
    - New 100,000 sq. ft. site, but only 20% utilized
    - One of largest outbound telemarketing firms

Those interviewing me said that they needed leadership. I learned soon that meant they had neither a clear vision nor a strategy. Further, they had a highly fractured management team composed of people who had been in American Airlines and had been moved out of the mainline business into this subsidiary, and a group of people who had come in from outside. Further, we had frontline employee turnover of over 200%.

We had state-of-the-art facilities, including a brand-new 100,000 square foot building, but it was only 20% utilized. We were in the rapidly growing and quickly changing telemarketing business, providing only outbound calls, between 5 PM and 9 PM. If you want to understand what a 100,000 square foot building with only 20% occupied looks like, think of a football field with a tarp covering one end zone and the rest open. Of course, you would have to really hone your visualization skills to see the 1000 workstations sitting there empty.

Obviously, the words used in the interview did not mean quite what I thought. Their vision for the future wasn't what I had in mind when I took on the "challenge." Our task, obviously, was to determine, "Where we go from here?" But before I do that, I want to reflect briefly on what Michael O'Brien talked about yesterday, the difference between aggressive-defensive and constructive cultures. From both the titles of these two culture types, and the research that has been done by Kotter and Heskett, we know that organizations with constructive cultures are far more productive than those with defensive cultures. The chart in Table Two illustrates the substantial difference in productivity. I can substantiate these figures after having used The Pacific Institute's program twice for building a constructive culture in organizations.

TABLE 2

Culture and Performance

Kotter & Heskett: Study of 207 firms over an eleven year period as reported in their book *Corporate Culture and Performance*

	Defensive Culture	Constructive Culture
Revenue	166%	682%
Stock Prices	74%	901%
Net Income	1%	756%

Obviously, building constructive cultures works, and that's what we started doing at American, but we learned some hard lessons in the process. It was a process akin to changing a flat tire while still driving the car.

With AADMC, we started with a vision. Why? A vision is something you start pulling people toward. People have to have a view or picture of where it is that you are taking them, and you have to keep repeating it, repeating it and repeating it. It didn't have to be a very complicated picture. It's just that we wanted to be "Number One in our industry, in customer service, in quality, and profitability." We knew that if we became Number One, we would return a result that would keep our shareholders satisfied. (See Table Three for the challenge we faced.)

TABLE 3

The Challenge at American - 1988
American Airlines Direct Marketing Corporation (AADMC)
- *Vision and strategy molded*
- Sales and profit still struggling
- Team not yet together
- Employee Turnover still over 200%
- Frontline supervisors lacking leadership training & coaching skills
- TPI recommended by Training Manager

Our next step was developing a strategy to fill the 100,000 square foot building, day and night. If you're calling only from five to nine o'clock in every time zone, you have 1000 empty seats all day long. And that's lost opportunity.

We had a team that wasn't really together, AA people and non-AA people. Employee turnover was still a serious problem, in part because we were paying just barely above minimum wage at the time. The most serious need was better training of our front line supervisors. We couldn't have a quality product or good customer service unless we had a group of people who believed they could do what was necessary to provide those necessities – and it had to start with first-line supervisors.

I told our training manager that we needed a program for first-line supervisors that teaches them the very essence of leadership, including the importance of such things as the leader establishing the vision and helping those being led to see their role in it; the alignment of the team behind the goals of the organization; and the importance of belief at all levels in the ability to develop a successful organization.

At this point, our training manager told me about The Pacific Institute's program, which she had facilitated at AT&T. I sent some of our best folks to take a look at the curriculum (called *Investment In Excellence*® in those days.) They returned encouraging me to see the program first-hand. So, I attended, while knowing that if we could really engage those first-line supervisors, we could impact turnover, customer service and quality, which in turn would attract customers.

So I went through the program. Needless to say, I was absolutely amazed! It encompassed everything that we wanted the supervisors to learn and more.

We then changed our approach and decided that the first thing to do was to get the Executive Team to attend The Pacific Institute program. The team attended the program and was very impacted. We had all seen similar programs in our careers but nothing as well organized and actionable. We decided that we would make it not only an important part of first-line supervisor training, but also the basis of all training in the organization. We also decided to refine our vision, to make it clearer and more appealing to employees. We redefined our strategies and made our goals much bigger than they were. (See Table Four)

> **TABLE 4**
>
> # The Growth of the Team - 1989
>
> - *TPI becomes the foundation for a new culture*
> - *IIE* basis for all employee training
> - Teams become much more effective
> - Sales increase as well as quality of work
> - Turnover drops to 100%
> - New business operation approved
> - New technology uncovered

Slowly, we were starting to see things turn around, and we said "What would it be like if we did a million dollars a month in profit?" And everybody said, "We're just getting to break even, how could we set our sights that high?" I said, "Let's just think about it. Let's keep a record of our progress to see how we're doing getting to that goal of one million dollars monthly." Month after month, we kept crawling closer and closer to our lofty goal.

David Sabey said the other day that good execution is also partly responsible for increases in business. Clearly he was right, but there was also our belief that we did not have to know all the "how's" now. We could just keep moving toward our goal, sustained and encouraged by our continuing increases in profit. The strengthening of our belief in our ability to reach our profit goal was mirrored by other benefits. We also saw better cooperation between our people; a better sharing of the common vision and language; and more interpersonal empathy. Barriers and hidden agendas began to break down. In short, the team began to come together. These are some of the changes that describe constructive cultures, which lead to more effective organizations and more effective means low overhead cost, further increasing profitability. So, we continued making the TPI program the basis for everything we did.

Over a period of eighteen months, two thousand people experienced the predecessor to *Imagine 21™*, the centerpiece program of TPI. We had sessions going day and night, almost twenty-four hours a day, seven days a week. Teams became more effective, our turnover started to drop rapidly, our quality of work and sales started to increase and customers' belief in us became stronger as their own results increased and our profits soared. Needless to say, "We were thrilled."

Because of our increased confidence and demonstrated ability to turn things around, we were given the opportunity to establish a new daytime business, which would lead to the full use of our building and facilities. Consequently, we got into the hotel reservation business, a primarily daytime operation that fit perfectly with our existing nighttime business.

Then, with the help of our Reticular Activating System we discovered a new technology at a meeting in Redmond, Washington. We did not know at the time that the presenter, the CEO of a technology company, along with his two brothers and parents, was a friend of Lou and Diane Tice. The CEO told us about a new call processing technology that would improve accounts receivable. It works like this. If you call a phone number and get anything other than a human voice, it hangs up. Obviously, this was a huge benefit to companies with large accounts receivable to improve the performance of their collectors. Now, it might sound like it is not that significant to our business unless you knew that our customers wouldn't invest in outbound telemarketing during the daytime, because they thought that so few people were home and we would spend all our time making calls but not contact anyone. They paid us by the hour, so calling but not reaching anyone would make it a very expensive proposition. But, if they could be guaranteed that they were going to reach somebody at home, they were willing to pay you by the hour with a premium to reach a new daytime market.

We invested heavily in the technology. You know it well today. You pick up the phone, you say, "Hello? Hello?" You hear nothing. Then, someone finally answers you, or then you hear the click that indicates the call has been disconnected, which means they don't have anybody ready to talk to you. It's called predictive dialing. We were the first in the industry to install predictive dialing. Over the next 18 to 24 months, predictive dialing became the standard in the entire industry. But we were out there first. We were able to use it, and get a premium for using it. We never would have found it had we not had our eyes and ears, and our Reticular Activating Systems, open to a technology that would solve a serious problem in our business. We set a new standard.

We started signing multi-year million dollar contracts with guaranteed annual revenue clauses, so that if there was a fluctuation in the marketplace, we were protected. We began expansion for new domestic and international facilities. Our employee turnover had now dropped to below ten percent, and everybody was working on removing "rocks" in the road. We had teams of people throughout the company looking at the little things we could do to make our business even better. We had the entire organization focused on goals. Our people could feel the excitement of success and they "bought into it, and bought into it, and bought into it."

By 1991, we had been in the process for three years. Sales grew over 100% in a single year. Profit now exceeded more than $1,000,000 a month. We set a new goal of $2 million a month. We established new offices in London, Brussels, Oklahoma City, San Antonio and Austin. Hotel reservations revenue had doubled. By the end of the year, the employee base was over 4000.

At this point, we noticed something changing. Our people were beginning to lose some of their enthusiasm for the values that we defined as a part of our investing in TPI's program. They weren't following those values. They weren't living them. We were starting to go back to old behaviors and old barriers started to reappear. We asked ourselves, why is this happening? Do we need to put everybody through the TPI curriculum again, or develop some other action? We asked our people what was different. We gained as much insight as we could from them. This helped us to recognize that just because we had a set of common values, opinions of what those values meant could be very different. So if we had a common value of respect, and we did, the meaning of respect held by our people could vary. We decided what we needed to do, in addition to defining values and other concepts central to our organization (and this is very important), was to indicate the behaviors associated with those values. This would be consistent with Lou's and others' definition of culture as "an aggregation of behaviors."

We further reasoned that if we didn't establish what we thought behavioral norms ought to be, how were our people going to get

TABLE 5

The Process that Kept Us Growing

- *Values broken down into behaviors*
  - Defined by the Executive team
  - Facilitated with TPI
  - Cascaded through the entire team
  - Refined by employees
- *Behaviors set as measurements for management performance evaluation*
- *Systems and processes revised to reflect values and behaviors*
- *Integrated with Quality Programs (IIQ)*

feedback on whether or not they are growing, or changing? This approach led to a long and sometimes excruciating process of defining the behaviors that were associated with the values we had in the organization. Significantly, everybody, two to three thousand of our people, participated in this process through workshops. Finally, we developed an agreed upon set of behaviors that we would live by throughout the entire organization. (See Table Five)

THE IMPORTANCE OF MEASUREMENT

It is obviously essential that we measure financial results, as well as progress towards our goals and plans. However, we believed it was equally important that we measure the behaviors of our leaders. In fact, we told all our managers that their performance review would include the measurement of the behaviors that we had defined through our workshops. We thought, "If we can change the managers' behavior, the people who work for them will emulate them." We felt employees wanted to know the behaviors that characterize leaders in order to become leaders themselves. We believed that this approach would lead to improved leadership throughout the organization.

This approach was initially unpleasant for management, because their view was that the measurements were intangible and subjective. We agreed, but told them that we were going ahead with the plan anyway. We put in a three hundred and sixty degree process, which yielded behavioral evaluations for managers from their boss, their peers and their team members, instead of a single dimensional system where their manager would determine whether or not they performed the desired behaviors.

We immediately started to see the behavior of the organization change. People had started to become accountable. We had raised the expectation in the organization.

Lou has told us, "We move toward and become like that which we think about." When you know that you are going to be evaluated on your performance, you are more likely to devote the necessary time and attention to what is expected of you. Immediately, performance starts to increase again. And we found that to sustain that, we had to change our entire system. We had to go back and take a look at our employee life cycle, the hiring system, the interviewing process, the compensation and reward systems, and all the policies that reinforce what it is that we wanted to have happen in the organization. It was a huge undertaking, and took much time to complete.

When we finished this important task, we thought, "We have everybody moving in the right direction. What do we need to do now?" We needed a standard set of work tools to help them solve problems. They knew how to solve interpersonal problems, but they needed tools to solve other issues and problems that invariably arise in any organization. To provide them with these skills, we created a program that combined TQM training, which we called Investments in Quality (IIQ) with The Pacific Institute's *Investment in Excellence®* *(IIE)*. We saw the quality of our work improve tremendously.

In late 1993, we reorganized the corporation. Our group was merged with other units of AMR into what is now called the Sabre Group, and was spun off from AMR. At this point, I left AMR with a tremendous asset, the knowledge of how to change the culture of a company.

Now on to our next experience in cultural change: In 1995, a partner and I acquired a small hotel reservation software company, Anasazi, Inc. We were the third owners of the company in three years. Not surprisingly, there was not a lot of trust on the part of employees.

As we started off, we had $11 million in sales, but it was not profitable. We had our work cut out for us. We had a hundred employees, mostly programmers, all in one location. We thought we could use

successfully the same process as before to increase the productivity
in this company.

We began with a new vision and strategy. Again, our vision was
simple: It was just to be Number One in our business. To do that, we
needed to be broader than we were heretofore. We already knew how
to run a hotel telephone reservation business. Consequently, within
thirty days, we acquired another company, merged the two, and became an international organization of two hundred and fifty people.
We then expanded our product lines. Sales started to improve, but
we were still unprofitable, and cooperation was still a challenge,
particularly between the people we had just acquired and the ones
we already had with us.

Having been through these problems before, and having been helped
by TPI, we once again brought them in to help us start a new corporate initiative. We went through the same process as before. We
defined our values, and the behaviors that flow from the values. We
engaged the entire workforce worldwide about our goals and values;
how we would reach those goals; the behaviors we expected to reflect
those values; and the expectation that we work together as a team.

We expanded our offerings and services. Our employee base was
now a thousand, with new offices in the United States. Soon we were
breaking even.

As always happens, competition appeared, this time a formidable
one, about twice our size. They were based in United Kingdom but
had offices worldwide. They were part of a large corporation with
deep pockets. However, the larger company didn't see its subsidiary
as strategic and decided to spin it off. We agreed to merge the two
companies into what became known as "REZsolutions, Inc." (See
Table Six)

TABLE 6

The REZsolutions Story - 1995

- Acquired small hotel reservations software provider in a leveraged buyout
- Third owner in three years
- $11 million in sales, but unprofitable
- 100 employees

REZsolutions was a small company by most people's standards, but it controlled about one third of all the hotel rooms booked in the entire world. Most people wouldn't know that. In fact, if you called many of the high-end chains worldwide and talked to a sales agent, you were not talking to someone from Fairmont Hotels or Forte Hotels or numerous other hotel chains around the world. You would be talking to a REZsolutions employee who was representing the hotels.

With this most recent addition to our business, we had expanded to two thousand employees in fifty countries around the world! What a challenge! We decided as an executive team that The Pacific Institute's *Imagine 21™ (I-21)* would become the foundation for the establishment of the merged culture.

Not surprisingly, as a fast, upstart young company, we had some problems. But our attitude was let's keep going, keep the vision in mind, just keep pressing ahead. We don't need to know the "how's" now. We're going to get there. The company that we merged with was a "how" expert. They had a 60-year operating history and were very structured in their approach to the business. We had a real challenge of how to get the "how" experts to see the big picture and how to get the people who want to go a hundred miles an hour to recognize that a little structure helps every now and then.

Again, we used *I-21* as our model. This time we took a slightly different approach. In addition to our own facilitators, we used TPI facilitators around the world to help us in this process. Again, we started with new values, visions, strategies and behaviors, all involved in the importance of defining the culture of the new organization. Our people understood what we were trying to do, and their cooperation in this effort began immediately.

We were ready to rock and roll! In fact, in the first six months after the merger, our revenues had increased sharply. But we were still a small $150 million dollar company, and in the dot-com era, that made you a target. Soon, we were approached by a dot-com company and our Board and investors decided that it was in the shareholders' and customers' best interests to accept the suitor's offer. The company merged with a public company, and is doing well. In fact, they now lead the industry.

THE IMPORTANCE OF A CLEAR VISION
One of the most important lessons we have learned is the great importance of a clear vision to the success of an organization. I ask all of you who are responsible for leading an organization, is your vision clear enough? I emphasize, is it clear enough? As consultants, we often see vision statements that are several paragraphs long. People don't remember paragraphs. They remember concise statements that create clear pictures.

ENGAGING THE HEARTS AND MINDS OF THE PEOPLE IN ORGANIZATIONS
Published and unpublished reports, books, and anecdotes point to the vital role of engaging employees in the success of organizations. Lou has referred to the obstruction that exists if an organization fails to engage its people. Melanie [Hayden, president of PartyLite Canada] expresses it this way, "If you can't engage the hearts, minds, and passions of your people, change becomes very difficult if not

fails to engage its people. Melanie [Hayden, president of PartyLite Canada] expresses it this way, "If you can't engage the hearts, minds, and passions of your people, change becomes very difficult if not impossible." It has been found that reengineering organizations frequently didn't work well because there was a failure to deeply engage many people in the organization. Ideally, everyone must be engaged, certainly not just the executive team. And when they are deeply engaged, they will do most anything that contributes to the success of the organization. They also must know that you have their best interests at heart, which, of course, means that they must trust you as their leader. A friend of mine once said, "If your people are engaged and trust you, they will go to the end of the earth for you." And they will.

MORE ABOUT VALUES, VISION, AND BEHAVIORS
The necessity of company values and behaviors deserves more consideration. Earlier we dwelled on the importance of behaviors accurately reflecting values. If they do accurately reflect values, there tends to be little if any misunderstanding of the meaning of the values.

Values reflect what it is you're about; what you want to create in the organization; about the importance of teamwork and the importance of pride in being a valuable member of a special organization. When values are defined in terms of behavior, they know what to expect. There are no surprises. Everyone starts holding each other accountable for what happens within the organization. It follows that when we have a misunderstanding about values, vision, or behaviors, we can discuss it with our colleagues in management, with the members of our teams, or both, thereby increasing the probability of reaching a constructive understanding about these terms, which are the essential elements of the organization's culture.

MORE ABOUT MEASUREMENT AND FEEDBACK

Why is measurement essential? A basic concept of the *Imagine 21*™ curriculum is the teleological nature of all of us. Unless we have feedback, we can't know for sure that we have the change we desire for our organization. And what's our biggest scotoma? It's our own behavior. Often we cannot perceive our scotomas. They can certainly obscure or distort our search to determine whether or not we are in agreement on organizational values. Feedback will reveal the answer to that question. And with feedback comes accountability.

SYSTEMS AND PROCESSES

Systems and processes reflect changes in culture, so they too must be changed to accurately reflect the desired cultural change. This is critically important. Kotter in his book *Heart of Change* contends that if processes and systems aren't changed, all the work put into building a new culture and a new belief in your organization will go out the window. People react to how they are rewarded, recognized, compensated, promoted, evaluated, and how they are coached. Kotter further states that if you're not living the values that are reflected in the underlying processes, your people will torpedo your efforts. We say "torpedo" because it happens below the surface, out of your sight. Every aspect of the employee life cycle must be addressed; from the day you start talking to somebody about becoming an employee to when they retire. Reflecting the desired change is imperative in every aspect of what your organization does.

IN SUMMARY

To bring about cultural change in an organization, the following conditions are essential:

1. The engagement of the hearts and minds of the people

2. A clear understanding and buy-in of the vision and values by the people

4. Systems and processes must be appropriate for the desired culture of the organization

When these conditions are met, you get lasting and meaningful change, and as Lou says, "It all starts on the inside." It's the same with organizations. Use the tools, hold each other accountable, focus on the Vision and success will be yours.

Progress, NOT PERFECTION
CO-OPERATIVE TRUST
COMPANY OF CANADA (CTCC)

By Myrna Bentley, CEO

Thank you for allowing me to share my story of very fundamental change in our organization's culture and success. I am honored to be on Lou Tice's stage. My staff colleagues are thrilled to be able to share the value of The Pacific Institute's (TPI) curricula with those who may be considering using it.

I am here to tell the story of the journey that we undertook at Co-operative Trust Company of Canada (CTCC) some six years ago. (See Visual One) It has been an exiting, occasionally scary adventure with opportunities for growth, not only for me personally, but for many of the people who make up this credit union company.

CTCC began in 1952. (See Visual Two) Credit union members needed access to mortgage loans and estate services. We were created as a credit union company. By the end of the 1950's, we had 140 members, and $1.3 million in assets. Not bad for a brand new company that offered only three products – trusts, mortgage and deposit products. Today we specialize in financial and trust services to a network of credit unions, deposit and mortgage brokers and a host of diverse corporate clients across Canada. (See Visual Three)

VISUAL 1

*em*POWERING
Canada's Credit Unions

CO-OPERATIVE TRUST
COMPANY OF CANADA

VISUAL 2

In the beginning . . .

- Incorporated in 1952
- By and for credit unions and other co-operatives
- Product lines included:
  - Estate Administration Services
  - Mortgage loans
  - Investment Certificates

Our business client base has grown very significantly, to approximately $13 billion. While we have grown our core business significantly, our product lines haven't changed as significantly.

VISUAL 3

Co-operative Trust Today . . .

- Specializes in business-to-business financial and trust services
- Primary product lines included:
  - Personal Trusts
  - Corporate Trusts
  - Mortgage Products
  - Deposit Products

VISUAL 4

What's Changed?

- Everything
  - Clients, members and the industry
  - Tomorrow, their needs will change again
- Co-operative Trust is "built to change"

VISUAL 5

The Early Years . . .

- National expansion
- Stable marketplace
- Diversifying product lines
- Traditional delivery

So what has changed? Everything. (See Visual Four). Clients' and members' needs have changed, and continue to change with increasing speed. In fact, we have become a company that is "built to change." We have changed the way we think, the way we respond, act and the way we see our future. To understand these changes, it is necessary to have a brief glimpse into our past.

THE EARLY YEARS

In the early years, our focus was to grow the business and expand across Canada. (See Visual Five) Credit union membership remained relatively stable. Financial legislation remained unchanged for years. Credit union members were content with status quo services and delivery means. We saw growth and progress in product line development, and, particularly in the late 1970's, we saw explosive growth and increased staffing levels to accommodate that growth.

We continued on our voyage, providing traditional financial services, delivered in a traditional way to traditional credit union members. We believed that we had proven that we knew what it took to be successful. However, we were only looking on the inside. We didn't look to the horizon. We had no vantage point. Then the 1980's came. (See Visual Six) Gone was the easy sailing of the previous decades.

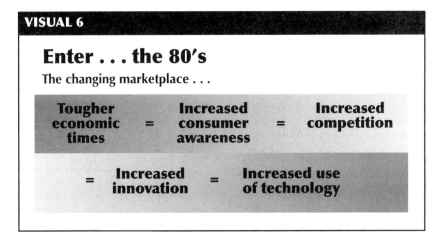

Tough economic conditions led to heightened consumer awareness, increased competitor and consumer demands, which led to competitor innovations more in line with the increased general awareness of a more technologically-savvy society.

All of these contributing factors led to a time of change in the financial industry nationwide. We, the traditionalists, the perfectionists – in the deepest sense of the word – were affected by these changes. We were heading for the rocks. A dramatic course correction was needed. So, we battened down the hatches, cut unproductive product lines, and implemented stringent cost control measures. We focused on the bottom line – we had to. We had multi-million dollar write-offs. These measures helped stabilize our operations, but our fixation on the bottom line and our necessary attention to day-to-day operations left us without any strategic focus to carry us forward.

The 1990's brought new waves of challenges. (See Visual Seven). There was no going back to traditional, comfortable ways of conducting business. Yes, we learned how to manage the numbers, the expenses, the margins, the risks, but we also learned that risk averse also means limited rewards.

VISUAL 7

What did we need?

- **Strategic viewpoint**
- **See new opportunities**
- **Set our course**
- **New measures for success**

Technology was breaking new ground, forever changing the financial services in Canada and, indeed, worldwide. Who can forget Y2K? Y2K consumed budget and significant resources. We were perfectionists in managing the business and the operations, but we were not leading the people.

A much more sophisticated marketplace pushed the financial industry even further, and in directions we had not anticipated. The financial industry in Canada experienced unprecedented competition. Our primary clients, credit unions, were exposed to the same challenges. Multinational financial companies offered more diverse products at a lower cost and with more advanced technology.

Credit unions began to evolve into highly sophisticated, multi-regional organizations. As they changed courses, so too did their needs. At CTCC, we were intent on keeping afloat, even in a whirlpool of change.

I was thrilled to become the President and CEO in 1997. However, I would be less than truthful if I didn't admit to being scared, given all the changes we were experiencing. My appointment was one more change for the organization to adapt to – being a new leader in a time of rapid change, working with vice presidents who had all been candidates for the presidency. But I also knew that we all wanted change, and that cost reductions and reliance on strictly bottom-line results could not sustain current operations, let alone allow growth desired by the company and our shareholders.

We didn't know how to think strategically, we had no business plans, but we certainly had lots of budgets. (See Visual Seven) When I suggested that we have a discussion about a strategic plan, the response I got was almost comical. Dennis Lyster, former Vice President and a great friend, maintained a sense of humor and appropriately described himself as having his head stuck in the sand for so many years that he didn't even know what the word "strategic" meant. It was like being on a leaky boat, paddling frantically, without paying any attention to the water falls ahead.

We were in agreement that we did not like the way we were, or how we treated each other. This made it possible for us to change. Consequently, the board and management tackled the hard questions straight on. Should we close the doors, maintain our current state, or initiate some changes? It was a scary evaluation process since closing the doors was a real option.

We decided that we didn't want to close the doors, that there was a strategic value and role for us in the market. Nor did we want to stay the same. Who wants to paddle like mad, focusing on the leak just to go over the falls and sink anyway?

We became committed to overhauling and setting a new course for the ship. We also needed a more strategic viewpoint, and to do that we wanted our people to stop concentrating on the leak in the boat, and to look forward to finding and plugging the leak, and ultimately, reach our destination. The question was, "How would we do that?"

We were already well managed, although in the old command-and-control style which created fierce competition between people, departments and divisions. Working together as a team was challenging. People's fears got in the way, which led to defensive and aggressive behaviors. Having lived in that culture for almost thirty years, and having contributed to it, I didn't want it to be that way anymore.

One of our first steps was to begin the dialogue with the executive management team. We talked about the future in terms of a vision or a dream of what our company could be. We asked them what they saw, and helped them to see what we saw. I learned that as the leader, I did not have all the answers. I learned that people respect you for telling the truth and admitting what you don't know, for asking for their input, and for being vulnerable. Ironically, I came to understand that the art of control is – giving it up. People want to help, and to have a say about the future. This was the start of the change, letting go of past behaviors and searching for the right tool.

We wanted to find a way to work together collaboratively, to ensure our leaky boat stayed on the right course and didn't sink.

I began to talk about leadership and people, not management, numbers and statistics – we were already very good at that. I asked my executive team to give me an opportunity to build the relationships we needed to move the company ahead, and to practice caring, concern and consideration. This was absolutely <u>not</u> the type of approach they expected. In our old management language, it would be called a "philosophical" or "soft" approach, not at all like the bottom-line approach to which we were so accustomed. Although they were skeptical, we agreed to give it a try and be better to each other by being more supportive.

Imagine how I felt. Courage was critical. Did I know what to do? No! But if you need a boxing ring, you can ask Lou, it really does appear. Here is my secret. I knew where the boxing ring was. Enter The Pacific Institute and Lou Tice.

Some months earlier I attended a small group session with two fellow CEO's and a few of their management team members. Leif Johnson, TPI project director was our facilitator. Leif was very good. The education was awesome, and I got excited! Here was something that was of personal and professional benefit to anyone and everyone!

I made the personal decision at that session that not only our company, but also the entire credit union system across Canada deserved the opportunity to experience this critical and valuable learning experience. I had no budget, and this program was in American dollars at an exchange rate of more than 30%. And, I was the only one who had experienced the education.

My management team had other expectations for education and investment in training and it wasn't TPI. I needed a coach to put the package together. I had the good fortune to meet Gregg Cochlan, a project director for The Pacific Institute. I am very proud to say that Gregg is a Saskatchewanian, as well as a great coach.

The Executive Management team bought in to the plan to use TPI's education, in retrospect, a critical turning point for us – for both

Co-operative Trust and personal perspectives. Our self-concept changed. I remember one of my first "ah-ha's." I was almost angry that we saw ourselves in such a negative light. We were like battered children needing a new view and experience. We finally broke loose!

It was TPI's education that gave us the means to constructively address our concerns, beliefs and behaviors. Consequently, we found that resistance to change melted away. We found new respect for each other, and became friends. In fact, I can say without hesitation that I love my fellow team members. That makes a big difference and it's very refreshing to know you work with others that care personally and trust you and can be trusted.

The Executive Management team bought in wholeheartedly. I had more paddlers and help to fix the leak. We were on the way to rebuilding the team, and we were excited to be doing it together. For the first time in a very long time, we were having fun, letting our guard down, and trusting! That was the beginning of the process, and our ongoing relationship with The Pacific Institute. The Executive Management team came away with a common language and understanding that the key to the future was people. We weren't silos. We believed that the collective "We" – management, board and employees – could see new opportunities and bring about needed changes if we were courageous, committed and trusted each other.

We defined our new leadership style as "traveling the high road." (See Visual Eight) We used six principles to define the high road: Trust, Compassion, Courage, Honesty, Respect, and Integrity. These principles are our individual and organizational affirmation. They define how we treat each other, and are the foundation for our maturing culture. We agreed that these principles gave us the right to expect co-operative performance from each other. Having agreed to this as our definition of our leadership style, someone suggested that we sign a document to that effect. It is interesting that they refused

VISUAL 8

Leadership Guiding Principles
Traveling the High Road

- Trust
- Compassion
- Courage
- Honesty
- Respect
- Integrity

to do so, because they believed that part of taking the high road at Co-operative Trust is that one's word means *everything*.

In our company, the six principles are found in many places, including the lobby, our mouse pads, and on cards, as a visual reminder, an affirmation, the HOW of our leadership commitment. These are not just words. We live these principles.

It has been an exceptional experience witnessing those six little words in action. We shared them with management and staff throughout the company. Every employee has an engraved stone tile with the Leadership Principles on their desk. Each manager and board member has engraved river stones. From the beginning, the meaning of the six principles has resonated with the staff. The overall culture has changed.

These principles are not always easy to live up to. I have made mistakes. We're all human. A staff member in a private conversation shared information with me that she would never have done before. She told me that at a meeting I made some comments that offended others, and that it wasn't like me. And, that she felt that she had a right to be honest with me about it. It took a great deal of honesty and courage to do that, and the trust that I would listen, and I did.

Sure, we make mistakes, but our spirit of intent is to progress, to be better, not perfect. This has become the foundation of our culture.

With this in mind, we established a staff leadership ambassador program with the staff explaining to new staff members the importance of the Leadership Principles

With agreement between the Board and Executive team, we stressed the importance of cultural change involving all of us together, what we refer to as the "open-mindedness of We" (See Visual Nine) as mentioned previously and stressed here again because of its importance. Because of this change in culture, we moved quickly from defensive behaviors into a much richer relationship between the Board, the Executive team and employees. Fears evaporated, thus enabling us to be truly constructive and to move forward together.

VISUAL 9

Changing the View
It's about the WHOLE boat . . .

- **Change – more than just individual**
- **Defensive "ME" to . . .**
- **Open-minded "WE"**
- **Beginnings of the constructive culture**

To assist in the next phase, we offered certified facilitator education to all staff in less than ninety days, whereas our original plan was to require two years. No one was required to attend. Instead, I asked that each staff member give a commitment of one day. Then if they didn't like it they were free to drop out. No one has dropped out, even though we run the program regularly.

Today we have fifty certified facilitators (I'm one), and new staff members are encouraged to take the course. TPI education was the key to aligning every person in the entire company, nationwide, for the first time that I can remember in some thirty years.

We helped our staff realize and affirm that we are truly committed to helping them succeed and that we each play an integral part in assuring the company's success. We affirm this approach regularly, in many different ways

We also provided TPI's *Purpose in Life: Ethics and Organizational Success®,* which also had a significant impact on us individually and collectively. As a result, we established a new corporate vision, "emPowering Canada's Credit Unions." (See Visual Ten) This was an intentionally bold statement, and reflects the company's belief that we exist to serve the entire credit union system of Canada. Flipping back to my boat analogy, it isn't just about the boat anymore. It's about the whole fleet.

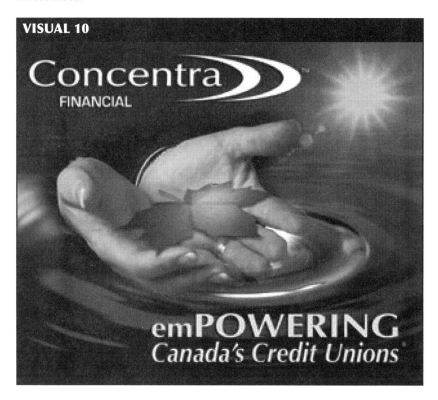

VISUAL 10

Concentra
FINANCIAL

emPOWERING
Canada's Credit Unions

It is important to know that amidst internal changes, we were running the business and making other significant changes. In fact, so much was happening, our Executive Management Team mantra became "Stay calm, Be Brave, and Watch for the Sign." This was coined by Dennis, an instrumental leader in this change story. Dennis lost the battle in his fight with cancer in late 2004. He was a highly respected and much loved person who had an enormous impact on all of us.

I can say without hesitation that I love the leadership team members in a very special way. It's more than a working relationship. It's a deep and important caring that we have for each other; we want to succeed together which is quite a change from the start.

Other significant developments include a joint venture with five significant credit union organizations in three Canadian provinces; a collaborative consolidation of technology services; and Project Genesis, another major corporate restructuring which will achieve greater capital efficiency, operating effectiveness and new and expanded product lines across Canada.

We have been measuring our progress over the past several years. For example, we have been measuring cultural change with a very reliable and valid instrument developed by Human Synergistics, the *Organizational Culture and Effectiveness Survey, OCES.* (See Visual Eleven) You will see that between 1997 and 2003, our culture has increased significantly from a low constructive style in 1997 to a highly constructive style in 2003, in large measure, we conclude, due to the effect of the changes we made.

This is significant progress; not perfect, but great. We are very proud of our people. Apparently the progress we made in a three-year period typically requires six or seven years. It is great to work in this kind of environment. We are also proud of the excellent results

VISUAL 11

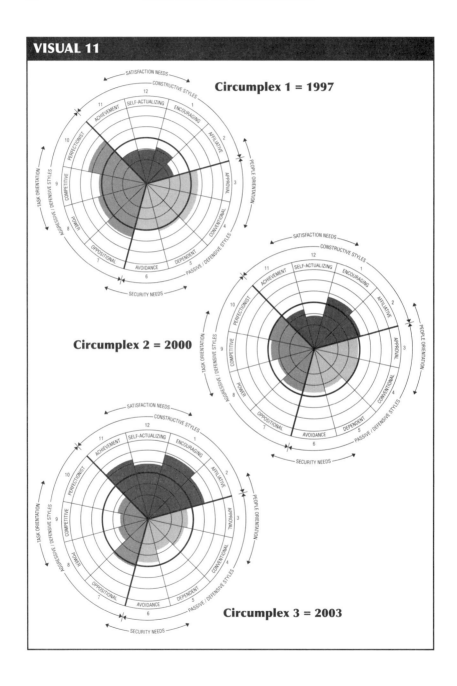

Circumplex 1 = 1997

Circumplex 2 = 2000

Circumplex 3 = 2003

of studies of our company by two highly respected independent entities in Canada, the Conference Board of Canada and PMV First Light Consulting Firm. We were deeply honored to have been judged by PMV First Light Consulting Firm, out of the top 100 employers in Canada, as the "Best of the Best" of the companies selected for the study. (See Visual Twelve)

These studies show how effective we have become in guiding Co-operative Trust to a highly constructive style. We are very proud of our leadership team. We have learned that inspired cultures drive prosperity and that inspiring leaders drive inspired cultures. (See Visual Thirteen)

What is the relationship between a company's culture and the success of the business? The financial results speak for themselves.

VISUAL 12

Measuring Success
Our Culture = Best of the Best

"Your ideal profile is inspired and respresents one of the best ideal profiles we have ever seen . . .

. . . There is very little gap in your ideal and your staff's current profile. This is an astonishing achievement."
—First Light PMV Inc.

VISUAL 13

Research Conclusion

"Inspired cultures drive prosperity"

and

"Inspiring leaders drive inspired cultures"

Profitability in terms of net income has increased 118% since 1999. Retained earnings have grown 32%. Productivity improved 11.5% reflecting our success in developing efficiencies and controlling costs in relation to revenues. In terms of growth, from losing 8-10% year over year to growing 12-15% compounded each year, 40% in 4 years. Employee turnover is less than 4%.

Our culture has continued to mature and evolve into so much more than it was. Our reputation has grown in the entire Canadian financial community, not just within the credit union system. When we began this journey, my intent was to create a legacy of leaders to carry the company forward, to grow the business, expand opportunities and bring balance to our workplace. It wasn't to receive awards or garner attention, or be in the media's spotlight. However, as our leaders began to shine, and we grew more successful, we have been moved to reach for even loftier goals. I'm not referring to awards, although awards are nice to have. I'm referring to the challenge of guiding talented, creative people to push their talents further, and creating an environment for people to reach their full potential.

The real reward is in knowing that, together, we've made a difference with a fellow staff member, a client, to our community and to our stakeholders. I firmly believe that it's progress, not perfection that we're striving for every day. Perfection is an aggressive/defensive behavior. We all make mistakes, but we take accountability for them and then move on. As a corporation, CTCC is built for change, not because of me, but because of our people welcoming change, instead of fearing it. It's just like us – just the way we are. My colleague, former Vice President and very dear friend, Dennis Lyster put it this way, "Ten years ago, people would have felt threatened by the thought that we are never 'there' (reaching the destination), afraid of looking for ways to grow and change."

So are we there yet? Absolutely not. In fact, we will never get there. (See Visual Fourteen) Things are always changing and moving. We have fun. We dress up, let our guards down. It's OK to be vulnerable. It's also OK to give in to the "softer" needs of staff: business and casual dress, earned days off, family friendly workplace.

VISUAL 14

The Importance of
Progress, not Perfection

- Journey doesn't end
- Don't expect perfection
- We get a little better . . . all the time, along the way

We have progressed from management to leadership. Now we are going to the next level, the Legacy of Leadership. We'll be discontent until we deliver the Legacy of Leadership.

And oh, that leak in the boat? As it turned out, it plugged itself. All we had to do was rebalance the load and head in the right direction. In fact, our crew has begun building a new boat. In the coming months, some of you may hear the name, Concentra Financial or Concentra Trust. When you do, think of us and know that we're still on our journey, and we're sailing along just fine.

Thank you for the opportunity to share our story. From everyone at Co-operative Trust, our heartfelt thanks to Lou and Diane, Dr. Spitzer, especially our coach, Gregg, and to everyone else at The Pacific Institute for this remarkable education, which has helped us make a difference individually and collectively. Thank you from the bottom of my heart, and the hearts of the more than 200 at CTCC who could not be here.

We're looking forward to another adventure on our journey, the Legacy of Leadership – Concentra Financial.

POSTSCRIPT

Concentra Financial and the wholly owned subsidiary Concentra Trust were launched January 1, 2005. The former company, Co-operative Trust Company of Canada, ceased to operate with this amalgamation. The company closed it 53-year history with all-time record performance in all measurements – both financial and strategic. The company was again a recipient of the 50 Best Managed Companies in Canada, a fourth year designation as one of Canada's top 100 Employers and received recognition for being a Community Builder.

Concentra includes the former business lines of Co-operative Trust Company of Canada along with newly acquired major lines of business. The company has tripled in assets and staff complement has doubled. The reorganization was achieved one full year in advance of the target date.

THE *Boddie-Noell*
ENTERPRISES EXPERIENCE
WITH THE PACIFIC INSTITUTE

By Mike Boddie, CEO
Hardee's Division of BNE

Today Boddie-Noell Enterprises is a well-known name in the retail food industry, easily among the Top 100 food services companies ranked by the industry's leading trade publication. Founded 42 years ago in Rocky Mount, North Carolina as one of the first franchises of the then new Hardee's hamburger brand, the company experienced steady and successful growth under the watchful eyes of brothers Mayo and Nick Boddie.

For a number of years, Boddie-Noell has been the largest Hardee's franchisee in the United States with some 315 Hardee's in North Carolina, Virginia, Kentucky and South Carolina. But Boddie-Noell is also a "well diversified company with a growing restaurant presence in several different categories in today's restaurant industry," points out Bill Boddie, the second generation of Boddie leadership and president and CEO of the company. Mayo and Nick Boddie continue as chairman and vice chairman, respectively.

*In addition to the **Hardee's** name, which is experiencing tremendous new growth thanks to the recent addition of the flagship product, the Thickburger, Boddie-Noell is growing elsewhere. The company owns the **Texas Steakhouse & Saloon,** a 30-restaurant chain in the Mid-Atlantic region that is a strong entry in the casual dining category. The*

*company also has launched a two-restaurant entry in the barbeque
category (**BBQ & Ribs Co.**) with plans to double the number of locations in 2005; the **Café Carolina and Bakery**, a strong North Carolina
entry in the growing specialty bread/bakery-café dining segment; and
Highway Diner, a 1950s-era diner in Rocky Mount featuring vintage
1950s menu items. Rounding out the business is the **Rose Hill Plantation,** a 200-year-old historic landmark plantation home and meeting
facility located near Rocky Mount.*

*Over the past decade and a half, the company has taken an even more
significant turn in diversification with its **BNE Land & Development
Co.** which has commercial and resort real estate ventures throughout
North Carolina and Virginia with plans on the drawing board for resi-
dential and commercial development projects elsewhere.*

*The company's latest new venture is the opening of **Moe's Southwest
Grill** franchises which today is one of the nation's hottest new concepts
for casual dining in the Fresh Mex quick casual segment. Boddie-Noell
announced in 2003 it would open 25 Moe's in North Carolina and Virginia over the next five years, but the company is poised to open even
more than originally forecast. The company's first Moe's opened up in
Greensboro and Winston-Salem, North Carolina and Richmond, Virginia
before the end of 2004.*

*Today Boddie-Noell stands as a major presence in restaurant circles
(the sixth-largest retail food franchisee in the U.S. in 2003, according to
Restaurant Finance Monitor). With more than 12,000 employees spread
across its operating area, Boddie-Noell ranks among the top five privately held companies in both North Carolina and Virginia in employment.*

*But despite four decades of growth and evolution in the retail food
business, Boddie-Noell has succeeded because of a distinct approach it
takes towards its employees. The slogan "We Believe in People" is of-*

ten expressed as a sacred value to the company and one that has been responsible for the company's success.

Bill Boddie points out that people are the most important asset in business and without the commitment and motivation of a large, extended workforce, success is unlikely in the highly competitive restaurant and food business. The second generation of Boddie-Noell, under the operations leadership of brothers Bill, Mike and Mayo Jr., has reaffirmed their commitment to a family-oriented business philosophy and operating style. As a result, the company notes a significantly lower rate of employee turnover than the industry average, and Boddie-Noell has also been recognized for its innovative training and retention programs for employees.

Nonetheless, it's not always been an altogether upbeat environment for the company, especially during the 1990s when the competitive quick service restaurant (QSR) category became even more crowded with competitors; with it came price cutting, menu realignment and other strategies to grab flagging market share.

Boddie-Noell saw deterioration in market share of the Hardee's name as well as a succession of management and ownership changes that weighed heavily on the company and its employees. By the end of 2002, Boddie-Noell recognized even further changes were needed to enhance its culture and commitment to people. As Bill Boddie stated, "We wanted to change what needed to be changed and take what was good and make it even better."

When The Pacific Institute began discussions with executive management, there was a recognition that a clear step-change was needed to bring employees and the company into a different way of viewing their relationship towards one another and discovering the potential that lies within both.

With the buy-in and commitment of executive management, The Pacific Institute (TPI) has become a real part of the business culture within Boddie-Noell. According to Bill Boddie, by the end of 2004, Boddie-Noell had introduced more than 700 of its employees to TPI.

Nowhere within the company has the introduction of TPI been more evident than with the Hardee's Division led by Mike Boddie. In late 2004 Mike Boddie was asked to describe the integration of TPI's philosophy in Seattle at The Pacific Institute's Global Conference. Following are Mike Boddie's remarks, delivered at the conference, about where the company was at the outset of its new relationship with TPI and the process under which it has been introduced to a far-flung and large workforce for this dynamic company.

The year was 1961; John F. Kennedy took office as our 35th President of the United States. I was four years old and my two brothers were ages seven and eight. Our father owned and operated a service station or what some people may call a gas station. My uncle was managing a small motel that he, my father and great uncle had built. Two blocks from my father's service station he noticed a new building being built. Two of his childhood friends had gone into partnership with a man named Wilbur Hardee to start a fast food restaurant chain named Hardee's. This was the second Hardee's being built. They asked my father if he would like to become a franchisee and build his own Hardee's restaurants. My father stated he did not want anything to do with the restaurant business, but he kept his eye on it, especially after it opened and people were lining up to purchase 15¢ hamburgers, 10¢ soft drinks and 10¢ french fries.

After learning it had great controls and it was a cash business much like his service station, he liked it. So he, along with my uncle and great uncle bought four franchises to build and operate Hardee's. They were the 2nd franchisee of Hardee's behind Jerry Richardson, who later sold his restaurants and went on to create and own the

Carolina Panthers professional football team. So, that is how Boddie-Noell began; Boddie, the last name of my father Mayo and Uncle Nick and Noell, the last name of my Great Uncle Carleton. After the opening of their first Hardee's in 1962, my father said if we could get four restaurants operating like this one we would be in "high cotton" which means Real Good!

So, where are we today? I think the easiest way to explain what Boddie-Noell has evolved into is through an orientation video we use for all new employees. What you would see is the different divisions that make up Boddie-Noell. At the end of the video, you would see my brother, Bill, who is President and Chief Operating Officer of BNE. He could not be here because he and my oldest brother, Mayo, Jr., are living out their affirmation today. They are riding their Harley Davidson's into Sturgis, South Dakota, at the motorcycle round up.

My father and uncle started Boddie-Noell with a simple philosophy that if you focus on your people first, the profits and everything else will come. It worked for many years. As the company grew, so did the layers of management with a lot of different personalities, which made that simple philosophy hard to maintain. I took over the Hardee's Division in the fall of 1995 and was disturbed to see we didn't have a strong backup of management. There was no development or succession planning in place. The majority of our leadership had been in their positions since the 1970's and 80's and some were still operating with a management style that was outdated. I knew we needed a change in leadership style to meet the needs of the 90's and most definitely 2000 and beyond.

We worked diligently to lead our people properly. We put systems of controls and measurements in place. We had the leadership team and we had the controls but we needed more sales. Hardee's had been a beaten up brand over the years and sales had been declining. We needed something to rally around – a horse to ride!

Fortunately, Hardee's had been testing a concept of 1/3 and 1/2 pound burgers that was on the way, but what about our people? We had put in place a process to identify potential new leaders and place them on a "promotable" list. We had programs to help develop them operationally but we were still missing something, something for the individuals themselves. We had tried several programs that just didn't last because there was no follow up. A week after the course, our people would be back at work doing their job and would have forgotten most of what they had gone through the program for!

Then, we got a call from Jason Wilkie representing a company called "The Pacific Institute," which we had never heard of. He told us that the largest Arby's franchisee, RTM located in Atlanta, had been using The Pacific Institute principles for years. Well, we knew RTM, so we gave them a call and they spoke very highly of The Pacific Institute, basically how they had ingrained the principles into their culture.

In the spring of 2002, Bob Crumley, our Sr. Vice President of Personnel and who is here today, came to Seattle and sat through an *Imagine 21™* session conducted by Jane McDade. Bob was very impressed, but he is a personnel guy and they like everything. So, he asked if I would come and visit to see what I thought. I brought my Vice President of Operations with me and we were fortunate to attend a 3-day "live" seminar with Lou. We felt the same as Bob, that this could be good for Boddie-Noell if we could apply it across the company. We went back and met with our Senior Leadership group, which Bob and I are on, along with Mike Hancock, Executive Vice President who is here today. Our Senior Leadership group is made up of nine individuals who oversee all of our concepts, divisions and support groups. We decided we needed to look at this.

Later in 2002, Lou Tice was in the Southeast and we were able to have Lou talk to our officer group of Vice Presidents and Directors and give them a taste of *Imagine 21*™ so they could get an idea of what Bob, Terry and I had been talking about.

The next step was to take this officer group of about 40 people through *Imagine 21,* which we did in Rocky Mount, NC. We were blessed with fantastic facilitators by the names of Leif Johnson and Christina Maddox, who with their high energy and great personalities got everyone excited and motivated. They are here today and I just want to thank you for what you have done for our company and our people. I'll talk more about Christina in a little while.

So, there we were. We had taken our officers through *Imagine 21* (last quarter 2002 and first quarter 2003). They liked it, but were they committed to it? We laid out the cost to do our company through the General Manager level and the time frame, and then we put it to a vote. This was not a Senior Management level decision. We had to be in it together. The vote was unanimous that this is what we needed for our people. You need to understand, at this point in Boddie-Noell's life, we had just come off our first year of decent bottom line results. That was only because of the controls and measurements we had put in place. The years before had been lean because of Hardee's performance and it would have been easy to spend the money in other areas. We had to have sales improvements but we didn't know when that would be. Everyone knew we needed to continue to invest in our people if we were going to move our company forward, so we said, "Let's go."

In the summer of 2003, we took our home office support staff of about 200 people through *Imagine 21*. In the winter of 2003-2004, we took our District Manager level through, which was approximately 40 people with Christina Maddox. These groups were easy because we could do it all in Rocky Mount, bringing them into a central location.

The challenge was to take it to over 317 locations, these being Hardee's General Managers; at this same time, we were rolling out the new Hardee's "Revolution" menu of 1/3 and 1/2 pound burgers. Going to 100% Angus Beef, cooking to order and delivering it to the customer at their table in the dining room in a fast food restaurant was the largest operational change in Hardee's 40-year history and a big change to our lunch / dinner customers.

(Our customers were not used to ordering at the counter, having a seat and their food delivered to them. But when they got it, it was excellent. We had kitchen changes with equipment and hoods. The menu was so complex that a District Manager could only roll one store per week. They would roll the menu on Wednesday and stay until Saturday or Sunday to make sure the store was executing everything correctly. Then, go to their next restaurant and start preparing for the next Wednesday. On top of this, we were remodeling about 25%, or 60 of our restaurants. Now, we were going to throw *Imagine 21*™ at our General Managers.)

Before we started our General Manager *Imagine 21* sessions, we conducted a General Managers Road Show meeting, something we do each year in March, where we go out into our regions for General Manager Meetings. At these meetings, we review the past year's sales and results. We celebrate our successes. We give a lot of door prizes away and we make it an upbeat, motivational day. We also have individuals from our support groups talk about changes to programs or new benefits that might affect our General Managers. Also, we talk about our present year, our goals and how we plan to achieve them. This year we gave them a taste of *Imagine 21*. At the road shows, we had District Managers, Directors, Vice Presidents and support staff share some of their successes so the General Managers could see the impact of affirmations, self-talk and goal-setting to build excitement. We also shared our Hardee's Division affirmation, designating a specific average unit volume per restaurant for the year 2004.

Boddie-Noell Hardee's had not reached this figure for over six years, as Hardee's had been in a tailspin but we were coming back. The last half of 2003 had been better and we were rolling the new "Revolution" menu.

Our Hardee's division of 317 restaurants is divided into four regions with between 80 to 100 restaurants each. Each region is divided between a Vice President and a Director to split operational responsibilities. Out of the regions, we basically have nine areas with about 35 restaurants in each area. To cover this amount of territory in four different states, we trained and developed 49 facilitators out of our home office support staff and our District Manager level.

We also felt we had one shot at a first impression on our General Managers with the first two days of *Imagine 21*™. We wanted to make sure our General Managers understood the power of *Imagine 21,* the impact of *Imagine 21* and that they got it. If we were going to move our company forward, we needed everyone speaking the same language and focused on the same goal. Our General Managers are the machine of our company and they would be the ones to move us. We asked Christina Maddox if she would be the lead facilitator in each General Managers first 2-day session along with Boddie-Noell facilitators helping and discussing a few units each day.

We wanted our General Managers to know that we believed in The Pacific Institute, were serious about it and that a professional would lead them through it. Christina was so good, because she traveled and did all nine areas, and was able to read the group and change up the program if a particular group was not responding. Christina actually went out and worked in our Hardee's restaurants and made biscuits. Our second 2-day sessions were done by Boddie-Noell facilitators only, and went very smoothly. We rolled out *Imagine 21* to our 317 General Managers across four states in approximately four months. On May 15, 2004, just months after completing *Imagine*

21 with the General Managers, we reached our average unit volume sales affirmation. We were there just as we said we would be! We communicated our success to all of our people.

We have sent all General Managers and other operations leadership gifts to recognize their accomplishment. And now, we have set a new affirmation on sales again, yet with one addition – Development of People, because without people we cannot do anything. We are well on our way toward that goal. Our people have grasped *Imagine 21*™. Some have done a great job, some have not, but that is what you work on. Our Hardee's Division is the largest franchisee in the Hardee's system. We are three times larger than the 2nd largest franchisee and most franchisees are very small. We are out-performing just about every other franchisee and corporate in the Hardee's system in average unit sales increases for the last 12 months. LIFE IS GOOD!!!

It was a tremendous team effort coordinating all of the *Imagine 21* sessions. After Rocky Mount, we had to coordinate nine different cities or towns, locations, meeting facilities, meals, snacks and overnight accommodations, while coordinating BNE facilitators that could go out. It wasn't like it was in Rocky Mount and a Director in the office could go facilitate a couple of units and go back to work. Our facilitators would go out of town for a couple of days. One of our facilitators here today, Kevin Boudreau, Senior Director of Tax and Risk Management, went out and facilitated to our General Managers and did a great job. Julie Taylor, one of our trainers who is also here today, facilitated a lot with Christina. Christina had her up dancing, which is way out of Julie's comfort zone.

We did all this while holding down our regular jobs. There was not one person who just focused on Pacific Institute solely. But, there were definitely two individuals without whom this would not have been possible, and they are here today. Patsy Daniel, Vice President

of Training and Pat Tolston, Personnel Manager coordinated everything down to the last detail. They didn't have a staff; they did it
themselves and did a fantastic job. The company and I cannot thank
them enough! During this time, we also completed:

- Cultural Consensus Building (CCB) = 10 Sessions with
  200 Participants

- Leadership Impact Study = Officers through District Managers

- *Pathways to Excellence*® sessions for both Corporate Office and
  Field. We have conducted eight *Pathways* sessions, in which Don
  Campbell, who is also here, has been very involved and instru-
  mental.

- Spouse program beginning this month (August 2004)

- *Purpose in Life: Ethics and Organizational Success*® is scheduled
  for Officers in September

- Lou Tice at Boddie-Noell Corporate Office in October

When asking our people what we could have done differently, some
comments were: "We should have mixed the levels of management
up more." In the field we did Vice Presidents and Directors together,
then all District Managers together, then all General Managers
together. In the home office, we were more mixed and got a lot of
positive comments of people learning a lot about other people in different areas of responsibility.

If possible, we would close the time gap, between when our officers
went through to completion of our General Managers.

I know we did a lot of things right because that's just like us. Present-
ly, all of our Senior Management meetings in Rocky Mount start with
a Pacific Institute *Meeting Starter*™. My monthly Hardee's Division
meetings start with a *Meeting Starter* followed by our affirmations. We

have given each Regional Vice President a set of *Meeting Starters*™ to use at their District Manager Meetings and General Manager Meetings.

Moving to the District Manager and General Manager level, we are developing champions in each region who, at least quarterly, will meet with a District Manager and their General Managers to review one or two key components of *Imagine 21*™ – Affirmations, Self-Talk, Goal-Setting. We will set this up in phases so the champions are covering the same components in each phase throughout the regions. This is one of the ways we will keep the momentum going in over 350 locations.

We have also created a steering committee made up of individuals from all divisions of Boddie-Noell to help maintain the momentum throughout the company. The Pacific Institute has given our people the tools, now our challenge is to continually apply them.

> It's like the story of the young man getting ready to go off to college. His father gave him a Bible and asked that he read it daily. "In it you will find all the answers you will ever need. It will help you, just read it daily." The boy said, "Sure Dad," and went off to school. He held down two jobs to make ends meet and have some spending money. He studied when he had a chance to, between jobs. After four years, he was physically worn out from the two jobs and mentally worn out from studying in between the jobs, but he scraped by and graduated. After he graduated, his parents went up to school, helping him pack up before he moved back home and before going out into the world. His father was packing some books and picked up the Bible. He asked the boy, "Son, did you read your Bible daily like I asked?" The son hesitated and said, "Well you know Dad, I was busy, things came up and I never got around to it. I just had other priorities." The father said "Son, take your Bible and open it to Genesis 3." The boy opened the Bible and there at Genesis 3 was a check written

out to the boy four years earlier by the father for more than enough to get him through four years of college.

The point is this, the boy had it right there in front of him for four years. He just had to pick it up and apply it. Not only would it help him financially, but probably spiritually too, based on his beliefs.

It's the same for our 700 people who have just gone through Pacific Institute that are responsible for our 12,000 people in all of our divisions, concepts and home office scattered over five states. We have to stay focused and keep what's important in front of them for us to move forward from being a Good Company to becoming a Great Company!

In closing – when asked, "Why did we invest the time, people and money in The Pacific Institute?" Remember – Our People, Our Relationships, Our Values, Our Beliefs, Our Culture are everything! If we lose this, our company is over. We will be no better than anyone else. But, we will not lose these because of tools like The Pacific Institute to move us forward.

Why did we invest in The Pacific Institute?

The answer is very simple ladies and gentlemen – because "We Believe In People."

Thank you!

THE *Winning Culture* IN ATHLETICS

Pete Carroll, Head Football Coach, University of Southern California
National Champions, 2003-04 and 2004-05 Seasons

Four years ago, I accepted the very challenging responsibility of leading the University of Southern California (USC) football program back to national prominence following a several year period of un-USC-like mediocrity. As in other types of organizations, a football team cannot excel without a culture that breeds success. My purpose is to describe the type of culture we established in the USC football program, one that played a big part of our being Co-National Champions in the 2003-04 season, and National Champions in the 2004-05 season. Throughout much of this chapter, the reader will detect the influence of Lou Tice and The Pacific Institute (TPI) in the development of a winning culture in our football program. In general terms, Lou's influence, in many respects, provides a systematic and powerful validation to some of the principles we've been teaching our players for some time. In other respects, Lou's influence has been more direct and specific. I think this distinction will be apparent to you.

I shall discuss several concepts that are necessary to convey an understanding of how we developed a winning culture at USC:

Directions (Goals)	Expectations	Thought Control
Beliefs	Self-Talk	Visualization
Authenticity	Team Conscience	Accountability

DIRECTIONS (GOALS), EXPECTATIONS AND ACCOMPLISHMENTS

The overarching direction of our program is to own the Rose Bowl. In fact, as we leave the practice field every day, we walk past a beautiful photograph of the Rose Bowl containing the words "Own the Rose Bowl." I don't use the word "goal," but I tell the athletes our program is based on the expectation of winning and even "owning" the Rose Bowl. They know that is our direction every year, and it will continue to be so, always. We also instill the belief that we will win the National Championship occasionally. I believe that if we instill a powerful belief system, important accomplishments like "Owning the Rose Bowl" will flow from that system.

BELIEF SYSTEMS

The concept of belief system as taught by The Pacific Institute is central to the development of our philosophy at USC. In fact, conveying in clear terms my belief system forms the core of my philosophy, which under-girds everything I do as the head coach. It follows that the more clearly I, as coach, understand my own belief system, the more effectively I can direct our program and keep it on course and focused. Further, I must have a strong commitment to these beliefs; so strong, in fact, that it must be clear that I actually OWN these beliefs. If I, as the leader and head coach, really own them, I will do a good job of emphasizing their value in producing a winning culture. The buy-in will be accomplished when my consistent passion and commitment to my beliefs are demonstrated in everything I do.

To illustrate the importance of a powerful commitment to the value of a belief system, the first sentence out of my mouth when I'm meeting with our football squad, at the start of the season, is "Our philosophy is all about the ball." Then I go on to explain to them that on offense, we *possess* the ball until we score. And we'll do everything in our power to protect the ball in terms of sound coaching technique, game planning and constant awareness of its importance. We do that with the thought that we'll never give it up. This applies to everyone – the centers, the guards, the linemen, receivers, the quarterback, everybody. That's the approach that gets us to a constant, conscious state of awareness about not turning over the ball. On defense, we don't play defense for any other reason than to get the ball. Our approach in coaching the defense is then directed toward the skills involved in the way we tackle, the way we approach the game, the way we set our sights and our directions. Consequently, everything is about getting the ball so we can score.

"It's all about the ball." This is as simple as I can explain it. It's the number one thing that I emphasize and think about around the clock. It pays off. We have had the best turnover ratio in the nation for the four years that I have been at USC. The first year we created 13 more turnovers than we gave up, the second year 18, the third year 21, and the fourth year 19, for a total of 71 for the four years. No other team in the nation can even come close to these turnover ratios. One other point about the importance of the head coach knowing what he believes and conveying these beliefs effectively to the players and assistant coaches: I know what I believe. I emphasize getting and keeping the ball better than anything I do for the program. Our success as a team validates the importance of this belief system: the National Championship in 2003-04, as well as 2004-05, and the most successful turnover ratio in the nation for four consecutive years. In the 2005 Orange Bowl, we were +5 in turnover ratio.

THE EXERCISE OF CONTROL – THE CONSCIENCE OF THE TEAM

Self-control through thought control, emphasized by The Pacific Institute and an important concept in Dr. Albert Bandura's well-known Self-Efficacy theory, is a very important skill we teach our athletes. We don't want our opponents to believe that they can get into our thinking, and we don't respond to what they are all about. We want to do what we want to do. We don't want to give them the satisfaction of making us react to what they're trying to put on us. This is an important mind-set that enables us to control what goes on; we do what we want to do and will not do what they want us to do. This is part of the "conscience" of our team. An example will help you understand how the conscience of our team works. One of our very talented young players reacted angrily to something one of our opponent's players had done or said. Just as it seemed to be getting out of control, one of our more experienced players intervened by simply holding his angry teammate at a distance. The experienced player did not have to say anything. The message came through clearly that we did not give our opponent any reason to believe that he was getting into our thinking.

THE VALUE OF SELF-TALK IN THE DEVELOPMENT OF TEAM CONSCIENCE

The value of self-talk in our program can be illustrated by showing how this skill is useful in our players' learning and living by the rules in our program. Rule #1 in the development of team conscience is always protect your team. This is about being a team, and experiencing all of the good things that can flow out of that rule. This rule applies to being supportive of the team when talking to the media. It means turning your thinking and attention to teammates, not yourself, and never to our opponents.

Rule #2 is all about self-talk. This rule is borrowed from legendary UCLA basketball coach John Wooden: "No whining, no complaining and no excuses." Essentially, this means that you cannot talk about things that bother you. You cannot try to sell your negative thoughts to somebody else. We are not going to be blame-fixers. Rather, we're going to suck it up and find a way to fix the problem ourselves. It does have to do with being mentally tough and not giving in to your weaker moments.

Rule #3 is simply "Be early!" This rule as part of the team conscience requires team members to be early to practices, meetings, classes and other events. Again, these rules can be learned more quickly by skillful use of self-talk. It is worth repeating that we consider these three rules to be important in the development of the team con-science, and it means that team members must be accountable.

THE TEAM CONCEPT IN GAME SITUATIONS

During a game, one of the concepts I adhere to is not projecting desired outcomes of that game. Also, I try to project our focus be-yond winning a particular game. I'm a real stickler about not passing judgment at any time during a game – that it is won or not won, over or not over. As a result, our guys know that you can't win in the first quarter, the second, or even the third quarter. Somewhere toward the end of the fourth quarter the game will be won, perhaps even on the last play.

Related to the above is our insistence that we continue to project in-creasingly challenging accomplishments. We don't allow the team to settle in on the belief that they have no more wins to celebrate, that there is nothing else out there for them. We don't allow them to think that winning the National Championship is the end result, that there isn't anything else out there for them. That kind of thinking could contribute to their never winning another National Championship. Although we beat UCLA and Notre Dame for the first time in twenty years, both in 2002, our attitude should be, "Let's see how many consecutive years we can beat them both in the same season!"

Lou illustrates this point by giving the example of goal-setting to get home after work when you're dead tired, and all you want to do is get home and rest on the couch. With that attitude, you will probably get no further than the couch.

THE POWER OF BEING AUTHENTIC

Our team, players and coaches, must know who we are and what we stand for. Our identity must be clear if we are going to be consistent and authentic. We demonstrate who we are every time we are on the field by the style of our play, and the way we handle difficult issues. The authenticity thing really makes sense to me in terms of an individual, a group and a team. If you don't know who you are, then you have to develop that understanding. Once you develop who you are, you must adhere to it consistently. In developing authenticity, self-talk is extremely helpful, just as it is in developing the team concept that I referred to earlier.

Our assistant coaches who have been with us for a while know about Lou Tice and that our program contains some of the key concepts of The Pacific Institute's programs. They also know enough to understand that the concepts we have focused on here at USC are important components of the centerpiece program of The Pacific Institute, *Investment in Excellence®*, and that, as mentioned earlier, the work of The Pacific Institute supports my belief that the concepts we are using have contributed significantly to our recapturing the winning culture at the University of Southern California.

LEADERSHIP

One final point of interest to me is something that Lou referred to early in our association. It is the distinction between Whiteheadian and Newtonian leadership styles. Lou let me know that I was somewhat of a Whiteheadian leader. At first, I didn't know about Newtonian and Whiteheadian styles. Lou told me that Whitehead, the philosopher, was more of a consensus leader and Newton, the scientist, was more of an authoritarian leader. This gave me additional strength and confidence to know that my leadership style is, and will continue to be, an important factor in our success.

We at USC look forward to even greater success in the years ahead.

Culture?
IN A CAR DEALERSHIP?
YOU GOTTA BE KIDDING ME!

By Mark Leggio, CEO
Mark-Christopher Chevrolet

I think it is great that all you people paid $995 to listen to a car dealer speak. And thank you, Lou for arranging for me to be the last speaker. I know that car dealers are at the end of the food chain. But Lou, would you please schedule me somewhere near lunch next time? That would cause my self-efficacy to leap excitedly.

We've heard much today about how The Pacific Institute's (TPI) curriculum can contribute to the development and the maintaining of a successful organizational culture. The concepts we learned from TPI's programs are rock solid.

The key is, once you've rolled people through the curriculum, how long does it remain effective? Are your people still working on the assimilation of the skills they learned from TPI? Are they still engaged? Do you continue to use the skills to maximize your potential? These questions are what we're going to talk about this afternoon.

First of all, when we started working with TPI, the culture of our organization like most, if not all, automobile dealerships was best described as hardball. We were tough, self-centered egomaniacs. We knew everything, racism was rampant, and diversity was absent. Our sales averaged about 200 to 250 cars a month, and even my mom knew that we should be doing better than that.

My mother told me one day that she had met a fellow named Steve Gandara, from The Pacific Institute, and that she wanted my brother, Chris, and me to meet him. I asked her what that meant. She told me that they talk about culture, mentoring, and getting along with employees. I then told her that I knew what our culture is: We're Italians. That was my mentality at that time.

To make a long story short, my brother called me soon to tell me that Steve Gandara was coming in that day, and asked if I could meet with him. I said "No, just go ahead and meet with him," to appease Mom, and me, and get this guy down the road. And I thought, we'll just get back to being our normal, ignorant selves, running our dealership, having half of the sales we're capable of generating. But I didn't know at that time we could be selling many more cars than we were.

Chris said, "No Mark, you can't make Mom mad. You've got to meet with Steve." So I said, "Okay, fine." At the meeting, Steve was going on and on about all this wonderful stuff. I'm thinking, "When is this idiot going to get out of this room?" But I'm being very phony and plastic – "Interesting, yeah, good, yeah." So I finally said "Okay, we'll get back to you."

So he leaves, and I said "Chris, I don't know what you're going to do with Mom, but spin this guy out of our life so we can get back to treating our people the wrong way, and under-living our lives."

So, Mom calls back and says, "What did you decide to do with Steve?" I made up some grandiose lie, because I didn't want to say, "I blew him off, Mom." Can't do that to Mom. She goes, "Well he's coming back out again, and I'm going to introduce him to Warren, our general manager, and I really want you to take a second peek at this. Okay?"

Well this time I'm so intelligent, I insist that I don't make that meeting, and my brother and Warren met with Steve. They ended up coming to the Global Conference up here (in Seattle) seven years ago. Whew, I didn't have to go to that thing!

They came back from the conference, and I'm doing what I normally do, which wasn't a lot back then. Warren was another old school, hardball guy like me, who came up in the good ol' boy system. That's the way the car business was then. Warren said, "Mark, we've got to have a talk." I said, "Okay, what do we talk about?" He said he wanted to talk about his weekend in Seattle. I said, "Oh, that Pacific Institute thing?" He said, "Yes." I said, "Fine. What's going on?"

Warren said he had made a decision in his life that this is the way we were going to run the car dealership business. "These are our principles, this is the vision, this is the philosophy, this is the culture, this is the new way that we've got to be running our store." I'm like, "Oh s—, he's lost it." He's a Bible thumper or something like that. I'm like, "Oh my God."

I deemed Warren so credible in my life. He's older than me. Although he works for me, I've always looked at him as a mentor. I thought if Warren is saying there is some validity to this, there must be. We get things pitched at us from Stephen Covey – all this namby-pamby motivational stuff that never works. But if Warren believes in TPI, then there must be something to it.

I went to Seattle, went through the curriculum, and I'll tell you something – I'm a religious guy, but I'm not overly so. I became a Bible-thumper with TPI. What I realized was, with TPI's concepts and message, we had a viable shot at being something special in my industry. Thank God, there are only a few auto dealers who have bought in to this. And I wish you would quit promoting it, Leif. (Leif Johnson). I like competing unfairly. It's very nice to think the way I think now, and to let those other guys with dealerships think like they did 40 years ago. It's great to compete with those guys who are clueless.

I knew that this was a chance for us to really make a difference, not only in our automobile culture, but in the lives of our people. I realize now that our employees were not objects. Formerly, I saw them as a means of making money. The real reason that my people weren't doing well is they weren't being coached well. After being immersed in the TPI curriculum, I started to coach and mentor the right way. The auto business is like other businesses. You must have the necessary skills, such as how to treat employees and customers, the importance of demo cars to the business. But these things become relatively unimportant compared to the following:

1.   Your people and your teams are all aligned to accomplish the same goals.

2.   Your culture values optimism, belief and confidence.

3.   Self-talk is upbeat.

4.   All members of your teams self-regulate at a high level.

It's much easier to be a good car salesman in a dealership with these values.

We disposed of all the untruths (I had a million of them) about how the business was supposed to be – remember, we were a 250 car-a-month store. If we had 200 cars sold after two weeks, I made sure we sold 50 the next two weeks. Did we have the potential now of another 200? Absolutely.

We took this message to all of our people, not only on the job, but also in their marriages, home and community lives. Now your people are armed with some of the best information in the world.

How do you get the momentum created by the programs of TPI to last? Much of what is to follow will address that question, one way or another.

When we rolled out the curriculum initially, we made a very clear statement to all 400 employees that we were going to change the way we did business. We outlined the changes we were to make.

1. We are going to treat our own people and our customers with dignity and respect.

2. We now emphasize the importance of coaching and mentoring.

3. Requests for confidentiality of any personal information anyone chose to discuss in the mentoring and coaching relationship would be honored.

4. Everyone must accept the philosophy, values and content of The Pacific Institute.

5. Employment at the dealership is contingent upon the acceptance of the four items above. We gave the employees the option.

6. It was emphasized that failure to agree with the above conditions did not imply any goodness or badness on the part of the person.

We told them that the information contained in TPI's programs helps people to improve their performance in whatever they choose to do with their lives – on the job, at home and in their community. We also told our people that with TPI's program they were better prepared to compete with those in other dealerships. It's very important that we told our people that The Pacific Institute's information was not a training program. Rather it is a way of life for our organization.

Having changed our culture certainly improved the way we did business and our interpersonal relationships. I have six departments:

service, parts, body, etc. and each had their own "fiefdom," their own kingdom. They were all entrenched. It was like I had six different wars. I spent much time putting out fires and "chasing the dog around the house," instead of doing something productive. Everyone was on a different page. Teamwork was just a famous word. It meant absolutely nothing.

Now we meet with every employee. I meet with upper management people, and managers meet with all other employees. At these meetings we develop a life balance wheel for every employee that indicates the values and goal components of the employee's life – work, family, community, recreation, financial, church, etc. Obviously, people are at Mark Christopher Chevrolet to earn money, but that is not all. They must earn money to fulfill their commitments to family, church, community, and the parts of the balance wheel. We cannot be a good coach or mentor without this information. In that mentoring relationship, our goal is to find out what is best for the company and the employee. In some instances, money is not the most important reason for working. Often employees want most to be respected and challenged. They want their word and opinions to mean something.

Now our company is into changes in organizational culture and team building, in order to be more effective, not just in terms of competing, capturing market share, and other bottom-line measures, but also in living a better life at home, seeing that your employees are buying their boats and new homes and being proud of the fact that through this culture change, the employees are legitimately happy.

But you cannot do this if you're *not* thinking in terms of your new culture. For example, at Mark Christopher, as a result of a goal-setting process, we went from 250 to 550 sales per month. We bought another dealership in a smaller town that was selling 19 cars a month. To give you an idea of the cultural environment at this new dealership, there were lice on the walls of the men's bathroom, rotary telephones, and bright orange carpets. In other words, it was a toilet. Bad!

My brother called me while I was on vacation to tell me that we over-paid for the store, because the guy set the high price, knowing what kind of operators we were. He knew that we could do a lot more with it than he did. When we got back to town, Warren and I went over to see the store. We were already committed to buying it. When I first saw it, my stomach literally started to turn. It's weird, after all of the education I've had and everything I've done in business, I was uncertain about how we were going to handle the mistake we made. It just goes to show you how one has to continually build self-efficacy and self-confidence. I was scared to death. My self-talk was, "We made a huge mistake. They're selling 19 cars a month. They're in town, while it is generally thought that dealerships should be on freeways." It was all coming at me, all the wrong information, and I was giving sanction to it. I'm sitting in the Taj Mahal down the road about ten miles, then I walk into this dump. "You can't do this. In-town stores are leaving. General Motors is buying them back." And I bought in to it. But I couldn't let my employees know that.

I brought my brother and four very talented, high-powered guys from the big store. We were sitting there talking, and you know, I was sweating it. The four guys are facilitators of the TPI curriculum. Two of them are the best coaches ever. They never complained about taking a demotion going over to this place. As they walked through the place, all they could see were opportunities. "We can do 30 used cars a month right away." Then it was, "We can do 50 cars right away." Then they started talking about the service department. I'm sitting back there going, "I'm supposed to be the boss. I'm supposed to be telling them that." My employees were bringing me up.

This experience is the most amazing thing that has ever happened to me in my 39 years. But can you imagine that you prepare your employees with the self-esteem and self-efficacy to where they bring you up? Who brings the owner up? No one motivates the CEO. But properly done, with the proper culture, and with the right spirit of intent, your employees aren't your employees. They're your partners, because you aren't working just for the money. They actually care about you and your expansion, because you care about them.

So we get into the store. It's doing 19 cars a month right out of the chute. In about two months, we had the store doing about 110 cars a month. Unbelievable! We got our money back in one year. I'm happy. Life's good. No worries.

Later I get a call from Leif Johnson. He told me he wanted me to meet a guy named Joe Atteridge. I told him OK. I'm an open-minded guy. I asked Leif why he wanted me to meet Joe. He told me that he had a program about the importance of culture in a business, and that he wanted my opinion of the program. So I flew to Phoenix to meet with Joe. At first I was skeptical about the culture thing. Then I thought about how important it is to check yourself to be sure that you are keeping an open mind. While Joe was explaining the culture of an organization, I was thinking that I would much rather be having a drink and a cigar with Leif. Joe goes through the program, and I said, "Yeah, yeah, yeah OK." So I leave.

Later Leif called me to ask me what I thought about Joe's presentation. I said "Oh yeah, you know, I'll think about it," as if I were talking to a customer. I also told Leif that I didn't need anything. He then said "Are you telling me that there is nowhere in your business that you have room for improvement?" I said "Leif, you just woke me up." I was doing 120 at the new store, and I was using that fact to confirm that I was great, and didn't need anything else. Leif believed that we were a 200 to 250 cars a month company, which we are now.

I am happy to conclude, along with other speakers today that the program that The Pacific Institute teaches will last if we "live it, walk it, and talk it." You don't run your people through the program, and then just sit around and fly by the seat of your pants, hoping to God somebody does something good.

Somebody talked earlier about the importance of business skills in the success of a business. I agree with that, but I believe when you think skillfully, it's a lot easier to do business. And I would much rather have the whole organization thinking for me than just me and two or three people coming up with all the ideas. I want the whole organization alive. And they are, because when they come with a presentation, they come to the table with something, we listen to them, and if it makes sense at all, we implement it. It will blow your mind when many of the ideas they come up with are so much better than your ideas. Having the whole outfit lively and thoughtful is the key to a successful business.

Thanks a lot for listening to a car guy.

Modern Terminals
A COMPANY IN TRANSITION

By John Yuen-Chueng Lee, Managing Director

Thank you for the opportunity to share with you our story of transition. I am not going to tell you about our container business. Rather, I am going to take you on a visit to Modern Terminals. To supplement my presentation in this chapter of the book, I am including some tables, or visuals, designed to make the visit clearer, and more interesting, For example, Visual One is an introduction to Modern Terminals. I shall share with you some details of the journey we have been traveling during the last five years in an effort to transform our company to meet the very challenging future.

We built Hong Kong's first purpose-designed container terminal in 1972. In spite of a risky start, we had 25 very good years in an expanding market. In the 1970s, Hong Kong was an important manufacturing base. When China opened up in the 1980s, Hong Kong's economy was transformed. Factories were generally moving north to China, to the Pearl River Delta area, about thirty miles north of Hong Kong, where labor and land were much less costly.

For the first quarter century, between 1972 and 1997, there was virtually no competition within the region. All cargo, including containers, in and out of the China region was routed through Hong Kong. At the

VISUAL 1

same time, the supply of terminal capacity was regulated through a trigger mechanism to meet the demand. As a result, terminal tariff grew every year with impressive profit growth. Also, we established ourselves as the industry leader with very high operational efficiencies. At the same time, we had become to some extent, complacent and unprepared for change.

In the mid 1990s, the competitive business environment changed. As you can see in Visual Two, turnover and profit started to decline in 1995. To some extent, some other profit measures started to decline in 1991. Then there was the Asia crisis in 1997. We were faced with increasing competition, especially from the nearby Zhanjiang container terminals, only approximately 25 miles from Hong Kong. The growth outlook was not good. All key business measures were "heading south."

After a long and successful past, we were caught off guard by some dramatic shifts in the market. Quite obviously, we needed to make some changes. So the change journey began in July of 1997. The first

VISUAL 2

1997 Challenge

- Asia crisis
- No growth outlook
- "Heavy" organization
- Shenzhen port emergence
- HIT speed aggressiveness
- All key business measures heading south

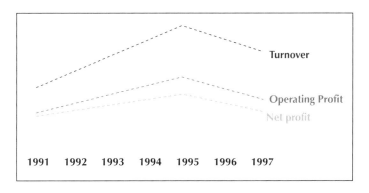

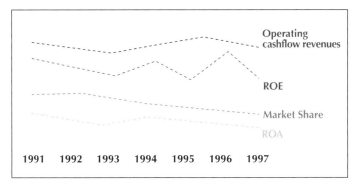

major project was what we called "Unicom," a bottom-up manning model, resulting in a 30% reduction in managers; a 21% reduction in management staff; and a total reduction of 400 of our managers and staff, from a total of 1800.

Additional staff were laid off and replaced by engineers who were more sophisticated, particularly in automation and re-engineering.

All in all, between 1997 and 1999 we experienced the biggest change in our history. By the year 2000, because of all these changes, we had achieved remarkable and very substantial improvements for our shareholders. Market share increased from 21.6% in 1997 to 29% in the year 2000, exceeding our rival market share of 28.6%. All downward trends of key performance and profitability indicators and measures were reversed and again pointing north.

In the spring of 2000, business conditions took a downward turn. Management thought the earlier period of good business conditions would never return. The good old days were gone; the comfortable business conditions of that era had changed dramatically and forever. Externally, we felt that we needed to be more responsive to our customers, and alert to the needs of the market. What is more important internally, we observed the increased nervousness among the staff about their future in the organization. Significantly, the cumula-

---

VISUAL 3

Spring 2000
Recognizing no return to "normality"

- Competitive pressure will be permanent
- Organizational effectiveness, innovation and customer services must be taken to new higher levels of excellence
- Change, change, change — "standing still not an option"

tive effects of the poor business conditions of the past three years seemed to have an adverse effect on trust within the organization. So now, the long march to improved performance began. We decided to turn our attention to cultural change within the organization. (See Visual Three)

The first thing we did was to create a strategic development process. We decided that it would help if we had the assistance of a consultant. We chose the Boston Consultant Group. We decided that we should begin with such issues as communications, mobilization, and creating momentum and expectations. We called a "stake-in-the-ground" meeting with the entire management group at the beginning of August 2000. We explained the purpose of the meeting, including the concern of management and directors over business conditions in recent months. We then set the stage for the next few weeks. Visuals Four through Ten are included at the end of this chapter (for those who want to examine in greater detail), showing the activities that were established as a result of the "stake-in-ground" meeting.

Next, we reviewed the challenge we faced in 1997, with special emphasis on the success we experienced at that time, and the good feelings our shareholders had about our performance. This was the beginning of our improved communication with our managers, shareholders and employees. Out of these discussions, we developed a vision and eight strategies for the future. (See Visual Eleven for the Vision and Strategies)

The Board approved our vision and growth strategies. The first two strategies dealt with internal organizational improvements and cultural changes. The next three strategies focused on our core business, and the last three emphasized growth through expansion.

VISUAL 11

December 2000

Vision

We will be the leader in providing value added container terminal services in our selected markets, to be our customer's preferred choice and to drive shareholder value.

Strategies:

- Maintain momentum to institutionalize a company culture that is customer driven, process and target oriented, team based and socially responsible.

- Become the preferred employer providing an environment in which our people will excel.

- Achieve industry best customer satisfaction.

- Meet shareholder expectations for profitability.

- Protect, optimize and grow the company's core Hong Kong business.

- Expand engagement in Shenzhen and Pearl River Delta.

- Secure a leading position in Mainland China.

- Pursue international position on a strategic and selective basis.

ORGANIZATIONAL CULTURE

As mentioned earlier, we developed a strong belief that one of the greatest barriers to the implementation of our strategies was the culture of the company. The core values, which lie at the center of any organization's culture, are well-entrenched and very resistant to change. Consequently, our first objective was to develop and implement a cultural change program. (See Visual Three) Again, most significantly, we came to a firm conclusion that to implement our new strategies for dealing with the changed business climate, it had become necessary to transform our corporate culture in such a way as to bring about a renewal of our organization. As the CEO, I am the leader of this objective.

THE CULTURAL CHANGE PROJECT

We carried out an evaluation of our own capabilities, skills, and the need for outside help. We looked at several proposals, but finally opted to go with The Pacific Institute's (TPI) Hong Kong operations. TPI specializes in cultural change and performance enhancement. We liked their proposal because it started with an individual and leadership emphasis rather than a system and process approach. We kicked off the cultural change program in January of 2001.

Why is the right organizational culture important? It is very simple. The entire process builds around these three simple but important relationships: Organizational effectiveness is the result of organizational culture, which in turn is the effect of personal and leadership effectiveness.

First, we established a baseline. We used the measurement tool, *Organizational Culture and Effectiveness Survey (OCES)* to identify twelve behavioral styles. We engaged the entire management to establish our vision culture, and randomly selected about one-third of our staff to identify the current reality. That means approximately four hundred staff members were taking part in the survey from the beginning.

Next we engaged the senior management team to formulate our cultural goals and to agree on our cultural values. Nine cultural barriers were determined by senior management colleagues following extensive discussion by all managers and selected key staff members. It was important that agreement on the nine barriers was reached by this leadership group. These were adopted as our code of conduct for running our business.

The Pacific Institute's *Investment in Excellence®* program *(IIE)* has turned out to be a key element in the process. Change is difficult. Many have tried, succeeding temporarily, then failed, and eventually they give up. What is needed is continuous and permanent change on the inside. I like the statement, "As I think, I am." It is our belief about ourselves, what we expect of ourselves, and what we believe about our ability to accomplish our goals that is so important. TPI's *Investment in Excellence* program is excellent for this important personal and organizational development. It is the kind of tool that delivers the cultural shift that would make the strategy changes possible. Over half of our organization, 650 people, have gone through this program.

Next, we introduced the *Leadership Impact Analysis (LIA)* program. This measure allows the leadership team to adjust the leadership style and implement strategies that are shaping the performance of others throughout the organization. Why is *LIA* important? It is generally recognized that the most important leadership performance tools revolve around strategies, skills and behaviors. TPI research demonstrates clearly that these skills are critical factors in determining leadership effectiveness.

The *Leadership Impact Analysis* is a very comprehensive survey with a very detailed individual report. The first part matches current reality with vision, and reveals the importance of leaders' personal balance and organizational and personal effectiveness in determining the desired impact on others. The second part of the *LIA,* quite similar to the *Organizational Culture Effectiveness Survey, OCES,* is more detailed than the *OCES* in terms of leadership behavior.

During the autumn of 2001, we carried out a massive communication exercise within the organization. It was a critical and major exercise involving the training of over 50 internal facilitators and trainers. They were all volunteers who would run internal courses and workshops. The two main objectives of this communication program were to familiarize our staff with our vision, strategies, and business objectives, along with the values and cultural goals that underpin them. The second objective was to help provide opportunities not only to know how they can help achieve all these goals, but also to participate in creating the way forward.

The early part of my presentation dealt with the 2001 business process. Again, in the subsequent two years, we went through the same process for the 2002 and 2003 business plan model. We achieved a better and higher comfort zone level the second and third times.

The subsequent two years, in the autumn of 2001 and 2002, we reviewed the status of the previous plan for carryover, and we will do it again this year. Each year's business plan and budget was presented to our shareholders. Thereafter it was deployed throughout the organization, and implementation was in the hands of all owners.

It was a huge effort, wasn't it? Has it been worth it? Yes. The numbers speak for themselves. The market share within the Hong Kong port was increased by 8.7%, operational margin increased by 12%, return on assets by 18%, and return on equity increased by 17%. Soft costs reduced by 21% by handling double the business volume. Fixed costs per container decreased by 62%, variable costs per container decreased by 36%, profit after tax increased by 47%, and the dividend distributed to our shareholders increased by 120%. (See Visual Twelve)

Has it been fun? Yes, particularly as you reflect on the total experience. But we must remember that to continue these successes into the future requires diligence in working on our optimism by faithfully practicing the skills that raise our personal and collective efficacy: self-talk, affirmations, assimilation and goal-setting, among others.

In conclusion, we simply picked the right time to implement the cultural change program, with the assistance of TPI Australia. We chose

VISUAL 12

Huge Effort — Worth It?
Key Financial Performance Indicators

	2002 vs 1997 Increase
Market Share (Kwai Chung)	+8.7%
Operation Margin	+12%
ROA	+18%
ROE	+17%
	2002 vs 1997 Variance
Staff Cost	-21%
Fixed Cost/ATEU	-62%
Variable Cost/ATEU	-36%
Profit After Tax	+47%
Dividend	+120%

the right program for our needs. We definitely see the desired changes in our organization, as revealed by the improvements in business indicators. We are proud of what we have accomplished with The Pacific Institute, and we are totally confident that the cultural change program will get us where we want to go in the years ahead.

Ladies and gentlemen, it has been a pleasure to be with you today, and to share our experience in bringing about changes in the culture of our company.

VISUAL 4

1st August 2000

Stake in the ground meeting with entire management group (40) "The Way Forward"

Agenda

1. Purpose
2. Where we have been
3. Current situation
4. What's important now
5. The way forward
6. Q & A

VISUAL 5

1st August 2000

Stake in the ground meeting

Agenda #1 — Purpose

1. Directors recent work on "company direction"
2. Set the stage for strategic planning process
3. Set the stage for business planning sessions
4. Management team buy in

VISUAL 6

1st August 2000
Stake in the ground meeting

Agenda #2 — Where we have been

1. 1997 challenge
2. **The organization meat grind**
   - You lived through it
   - You know the impacts — good and bad
   - The experience has become a significant part of today's company culture
3. **Positive results**
4. **Change, change and more change**
   - Necessary steps, but positive results
   - Where has it left us considering
     - Company culture?
     - Work environment?
     - Team health?
     - Employee satisfaction and effectiveness?
   - Are we positioned for future challenges?
   - What are the Phase II transformation issues?

VISUAL 7

1st August 2000

Stake in the ground meeting

Agenda #3 — Current situation

1. **Recovery on behalf of shareholders**
   - In good to great shape with positive outlook

2. **Company culture in transition**
   - Are we as healthy as we look?

3. **Company future under review**
   - The right time for self-assessment

VISUAL 8

1st August 2000

Company culture in transition — Are we healthy as we look?

Old	Current	Desired
• Fatherly	• Read the boss	• Open and thinking
• Centralized	• Cautious to anxious	• Empowered
• Factionalized	• Protect turf/self	• Coordinated
• Risk averse	• Meet expectaions/ no more	• Risk takers
• Protectionist	• Agree but not me	• Strategic (growth)
• Complacent	• Unsure	• Aggressive
• Satisfied	• Confused	• Continuous improvement
• Internally focused		• Operational excellence and customer focus

VISUAL 9

1st August 2000
Stake in the ground meeting

Agenda #4 — What's important now

1. **Organizational stability**
   - Commit to the management team
   - Energize organization around new BP objectives
   - Communicate priorities and resource requirement

2. **Establish a vision statement and strategies**
   - Management team involvement
   - Director's consensus
   - Wharf and Board approval

3. **Establish a business planning process**
   - Tie directly to individual KPI contracts
   - Commit to it as the way the company directs its business

4. **Institutionalize the company culture we want**
   - Include company values (cultural foundation)
   - Principles (underlying business philosophy)
   - Work practices (essential behaviors)

5. **Establish a comprehensive employee development plan**
   - Build resources for growth
   - Core training to create "one" company

6. **Establish and commit to an ongoing communication initiative**
   - Ensure no gap between leadership and the team
   - Ensure expectations are understood
   - Ensure continuous feedback and involvement

VISUAL 10

1st August 2000
Stake in the ground meeting

Agenda #5 — The Way Forward

1. Strategic thinking group as facilitator
2. Begins 3rd August through December
3. Interactive process to develop vision and strategies
4. Establish disciplines to set as our primary management process on an ongoing basis
5. Year 2001 business plan as deliverable

Transforming
FROM THE INSIDE OUT:
CL&P's COURSE IN EXCELLENCE

Leon (Lee) Olivier, President and Chief Operating Officer,
The Connecticut Light and Power Company,
The Northeast Utilities System, Berlin, Connecticut
Terry Lombardi and David Radanovich

WELCOME TO CL&P

On September 10, 2001, Cheryl Grisé, president of the Utility Group
of Northeast Utilities, introduced Lee Olivier as Connecticut Light
and Power's (CL&P) new president and chief operating officer. CL&P,
Connecticut's largest electric utility, provides electric service to
nearly 1.2 million customers in 149 cities and towns. It is the largest
regulated operating business within the Northeast Utilities System
(NU), with 2,300 employees.

Lee's charge was to transform CL&P from a good, traditional electric
utility into a top-performing, dynamic electric distribution business.
A set of binders, containing a great deal of benchmarking data, illustrated the size of his challenge. Nevertheless, this was a challenge
Cheryl and NU Chairman and CEO Mike Morris were confident Lee
could meet.

Their confidence stemmed from their first-hand experience with the
impressive turnaround Lee led during his three years as senior vice
president and chief nuclear officer at NU's Millstone nuclear plant and
from his 29 years with Boston Edison. They knew Lee's efficacious
nature was predicated on his inside-out approach – his belief that all

success starts with the individual. Developing efficacy on the individual level brings exponential returns to the organization as a whole.

This philosophy is consistent with the tenets of the *Imagine 21*™ program, which is why Lee saw it as an enabling tool for changing CL&P's culture.

THE CASE FOR CHANGE

Lee's first couple of weeks were an inquiry marathon. While the binders provided essentially a "due diligence" of the organization, company financials, operational issues, customer data, and organizational charts, Lee wanted to understand how the organization functioned – what were the business and cultural drivers of performance. Questioning, listening and personal observations became key in understanding the organization, its leadership style, how decisions were made, the actions/behaviors/results that were rewarded, the work environment and the organization's capability and capacity for change. He met with key stakeholders including customers, employees, the bargaining units, the regulatory bodies and the financial community. Within the first month, the hard realities emerged.

Internally, what Lee found was a process-based organization with seemingly satisfactory performance, but without a clear vision, direction and strategy. The irony of it was that while the organizational charts and people's titles included the name of the processes, the actual documented processes did not exist. Procedures, for the most part, were informal and based on tribal knowledge. In some areas where dated formal procedures did exist, there was a reluctance to hold people accountable for not following a procedure.

This was a risk-averse culture, centered around maintaining the status quo. This is not to say that there were not performance bright spots, but these were often not cohesive, nor tied into an overall strategy, nor executed with precision.

Decision-making was slow and it was difficult to identify who was accountable for driving performance and achieving stakeholder results. In general, the field workforce waited for guidance and permission to act from corporate staff. As might be expected, the centralized staff governance and CL&P's implementation of a process structure were barriers for achieving the strategy to become a top-performing business accountable for customer and shareholder satisfaction.

Much of the company's assets such as poles and wires were more than 40 years old and beyond or approaching the end of their useful lives. Nearly 40 percent of CL&P's skilled workers would be eligible to retire within five years, and it takes four-plus years to fully train and qualify an electric lineman.

With a history of over 100 years and a workforce with an average service tenure of 20 years, this was an organization whose members carried deep, taken-for-granted assumptions, beliefs, perceptions and behaviors. The long-standing relationships created an unspoken expectation to avoid conflict, and disagreement. Entitlement and a maternal expectation that the company would "take care of" the employee were pervasive. Effort, time and activities were as important as results achieved.

Externally, the restructuring of the electrical energy industry in Connecticut had caused NU to divest its power-generating assets. While CL&P's distribution business remained regulated at the state level, transmission was now regulated at the federal level. More of the services provided were becoming contestable. This meant CL&P needed to be prepared for other competitive companies, which believed they could deliver better quality and greater efficiency at a lower cost, and compete for services such as billing, metering and street lighting. Financial pressures were increasing because of capped rates at the 1996 level, through 2003, and the increasing operating costs.

Within his first 30 days, several things became very clear to Lee:

- To build a "best of the best" company, CL&P needed to be "unfrozen" and re-energized.

- The business needed to identify the key result areas, establish mile markers and the corresponding metrics.

- The organization needed injections of self-confidence, optimism, innovative thinking, realism and focus.

- It needed to build new relationships with the customers, the public and regulatory agencies.

- It needed the right people, individually and collectively, focusing on the right things at the right time.

- It needed new role models capable of creating and facilitating the transformational change from the inside out.

The conclusion was obvious. For the long-term best interests of the company and its customers, CL&P needed to be transformed into a company with a shared vision and a sense of urgency. CL&P began the transformation with a new organizational structure, the selection of a new leadership team, the implementation of new key result areas, a new performance measurement system, communication of the new direction and training to reinforce a new set of expected behaviors and beliefs.

LEE'S CHANGE PRINCIPLES

All eyes were on what Lee Olivier would do. He knew to change this organization it would take an inside-out approach. The questions he faced included:

- How can I help the people to see the best in themselves?

- How can I help create positive energy?

- How can I help develop a company that sees its potential?

- How can I help our company continually strive to be the best?

The answer: It would all have to start with Lee – his values and beliefs.

Lee's own values and beliefs would serve as guideposts for his perceptions, decisions and actions, which in turn would contribute to building a high-performing culture. The demonstration of these values and beliefs first appeared in Lee's written and face-to-face communications. Before too long, employees could see "the walk" matched "the talk" as the organization delivered on its promises, visions and expectations. Through the following change principles, Lee Olivier essentially became an example who gave meaning to "the new" CL&P.

START FROM THE INSIDE OUT
"It's not what you know and what skills you have, but what you can use of what you know in strange, unusual and difficult circumstances."

He knew from prior experience that individual efficacy could build into a critical mass. Lee had learned that to be successful an organization needs a critical mass of people who understand the reasons for and embrace change. He believed if people could realize the benefits of changing their beliefs and behaviors, it would change the culture of the organization.

It was important to provide the people with a means to assess and improve their own capabilities in a non-threatening way that could be applied to both their personal and work lives, thus allowing them to see themselves safely into the future. This was a situation where you draw on what you know and where you have been: a tried-and-true approach. So Lee introduced CL&P to Lou Tice's *Imagine 21*™. From personal experience, Lee knew that this program was effective in helping participants change for the better by seeing their own possibilities.

LISTEN AND SEEK TO UNDERSTAND

This belief can be attributed to Lee's first job in the energy industry. His job was to clean out the slag from the boilers that burned sulfur and coal. "The supervisors told you what to do. They weren't interested in your ideas. It gave me a good lesson about working in an organization where top-down management is the rule," Lee reflects. "All the good ideas don't need to be invented. They are already out there in people's minds. All managers need to do is get people together and listen."

During this inquiry marathon, stories about Lee writing on index cards began to leak out. In many different forums, you could see him listening attentively, asking questions and then reaching into his shirt pocket, pulling out an index card and writing.

These cards were multifunctional and served Lee well. They captured his learnings, ideas, affirmations, and critical follow-up items. Collectively they contributed to the development of CL&P's vision, strategies, and to determining initial areas requiring later focus and action.

ORGANIZATIONAL TRANSFORMATION BEGINS WITH LEADERSHIP

"Leaders embed and transmit culture by what they pay attention to, measure and control on a regular basis. New beliefs, values and assumptions are brought in by new members and leaders," states Edgar Schein.

The people holding top leadership positions must be aligned to achieve the desired future, results and culture. Combining this principle with bringing forward (and respecting) the best from the past, Lee's first critical decision was to select a new executive leadership team. He needed an officer team committed to the change, loyal to a shared vision and aligned with his guiding principles.

This radical change would require a senior team to objectively assess the current state, explore possibilities, and to make the difficult decisions and establish actions to not only survive, but also thrive under a new and more complex set of business conditions.

A rigorous selection process was cascaded down from the officer level to manager level. Candidates were evaluated through assessment center evaluations, interviews and collaborative meetings that explored their capabilities and qualifications. Selection criteria focused on leadership qualities, the ability to direct a work group, a demonstrated commitment to continuous improvement and recommendations from the candidate's supervisors.

One of the first tasks of the new officer team was to create the organization's mission, vision and values. Several weeks later, all the newly selected directors and the officers met and openly described what the "New CL&P" would look like in five years. This became the first step toward building the CL&P leadership coalition for change.

For many, it was a strange place to be. A vision significantly different from current reality, one that would be a significant challenge to achieve, can be scary and challenging.... at least at first.

MATCH STRUCTURE TO STRATEGY

To bring service delivery closer to the customer and establish ownership and accountability for results versus activity, the process-based organization was replaced with a function-based structure with three vice presidents. The Customer Relations organization focuses on all aspects of operation as they touch the customer and provides CL&P with a clear understanding of customers' ever-changing needs and expectations. The Customer Operations department is charged with efficiently executing the company's day-to-day operations to ensure that power keeps flowing to customers. The Energy Delivery Services organization provides for the efficient and strategic management of CL&P's distribution infrastructure, including engi-

neering and construction of the distribution system, and maintenance of substations and facilities.

Together, the new officer team was asked to optimize performance of
the customer service delivery functions by transferring best practices and establishing consistent policies and procedures throughout
the entire company. The goal was to create ownership for the people
who work in each of these departments for all aspects of CL&P's operations: safety, reliability and financial performance. This structure
also provided customer focus, common goals, clear accountability
for the employees and the customers, and a means for people's ideas
to surface vertically.

FOUR STRATEGIES FOR A
SUCCESSFUL INSIDE-OUT TRANSFORMATION

Having determined the need to change the culture of CL&P, Lee
leveraged the previously highlighted change principles to "unfreeze"
the corporate culture. To move the organization forward, he utilized
four primary strategies. Each strategy is consistent with not only
Lee's change principles, but also with the philosophical foundation
of Lou Tice and The Pacific Institute – utilizing key result areas that
drive success as the focus of organizational change.

1. **Invest in people – give them the tools to succeed both
    personally and professionally**

Lee started several communication pieces in the early months with,
"It all starts with people." He went on to explain, "As we transform
CL&P to a best-of-best company, we are committed to providing
developmental opportunities to every member of CL&P. I fully sub-
scribe to the theory that if you don't invest in your people, you won't
get the full value from your other expenditures."

Seeing the possibilities

"My goal is to spread new beliefs that create hope and action within every person, team and the organization as a whole," Lee explained.

Fundamentally, Lee believes that successful individuals breed successful companies. To bring personal and collective efficacy in the organization, Lou Tice's *Imagine 21*™ training program was offered to employees and their spouses or significant others. Its concepts and philosophies were aligned with Lee's personal values and change principles. From his prior experience with the program at the Millstone plant, Lee saw it as a major contributor in moving the plant toward a high-performance organization. It gave employees a framework for personal change and served as a launch pad for organizational change.

Through the self-discovery afforded by the training, participants were equipped with new lenses for viewing the world – for seeing the endless possibilities. Once exposed to the power of affirmations and positive self-talk, the people of CL&P began visualizing a future for the company that was fueled by imagining the best possible future on the personal level, and continually pushing oneself to improve.

As one astute participant observed, *"Imagine 21 has nothing to do with the company, and then again it has everything to do with the company."* Another explained, *"Imagine 21 has helped me focus. I took the balance wheel back to my work group and created one for my team."*

Continuously Learn and Improve

To effectively grow to new levels of performance, Lee believed continuous improvement and learning were core requirements for individuals and the organization. He felt true learning organizations seek to expand their knowledge base, to learn from their own past experiences, and to actively experiment with new approaches. Most importantly, they never assume that the status quo is good enough. His personal commitment to life-long learning is evident by the ever-changing stacks of books on his desk.

After major events including storms, "Lessons Learned" sessions are held. Periodic assessments are conducted by the senior leadership team to discuss what is working, what is not, and to develop action plans to improve performance.

TRAINING

In addition to offering *Imagine 21*™ to all employees, a new leadership training program, the Leadership Academy, was launched. It brought together all levels of leadership from the supervisor and up, and focused on leadership development, business acumen and alignment around CL&P's direction. However, this initiative served many purposes besides training. It formally served as a leadership rite of passage and challenged the attendees to fully commit to their leadership roles. It affirmed the belief that they were the key to creating a new CL&P. Furthermore, it provided a networking experience for leaders to share their best practices with each other and senior management.

Leadership development was not the only training need of the organization. Revamping the technical training was also a high priority for improving performance. CL&P developed an improvement plan that focused on establishing strong ownership of the training programs by the front-line organization, and improving the programmatic implementation and conduct of training, facilities, tools and equipment. Curriculum advisory committees made up of management and physical workers were established and significantly improved the content and hands-on approach to training. Clear expectations on the development of lesson plans, the conduct of training and the completion of training records continued with the improvement of the training process. The investment of capital dollars in the training facility, tools and equipment brought CL&P in alignment with similar distribution utilities' training programs and provided the necessary equipment to conduct realistic, hands-on training.

COMMUNICATIONS AND THE "IN FOCUS" STRATEGY DOCUMENT

To give the organization direction, and focus a one-year strategy document, "CL&P In Focus 2002" was developed and communicated by the newly selected leadership team to every employee. Besides communicating CL&P's new mission, vision and values, it clearly laid out what needed to be accomplished and identified how the organization would measure progress. Performance targets were established and a balanced scorecard approach was incorporated into what CL&P refers to as its Performance Enhancement System.

The "In Focus" document ended up being much more than a one-year plan. It served as the blueprint for CL&P's transformation to a best-of-best company. It gave purpose and team identity to all employees. It provided common language. Because it was hand delivered by leadership and reviewed in a cascading series of face-to-face meetings, it provided alignment for the leadership team and employees. It also gave leadership a tool and an opportunity to discuss the company's direction, listen to the employees, and to engage in constructive, robust dialogue. Building on the proliferation of the *Imagine 21*™ concepts, the 2003 "In Focus" document incorporated an affirmation for each key result area.

2. Set high standards/expectations – strive for excellence to realize your full potential

Beyond its value as a communication vehicle, the "In Focus" document set the bar for CL&P's performance. By titling the 2003 edition, "Delivering Results," the organization was challenged to take performance up to the next level.

VISUALIZE THE END GAME – SET A VISION – SET A GOAL

Lee often said "Begin with the end and state where you want to go, be, or do, and then you will find the way." He also believed that leaders should provide stories and pictures to help people visualize themselves as part of that future.

Consequently, he began describing the new CL&P with affirming thoughts and pictures of the future. During his first all-hands leadership meeting, his affirming scenarios included others in the industry visiting CL&P to learn from it; state-of-the-art work centers with the latest technology; lineman driving new yellow trucks; and all levels of employees working together solving business problems.

One manager explained this new way of looking at the business: "Now there is a focus on delivering the results. It's keeping your eye on the finish line – the end game and then you'll figure out how you are going to get there."

HOLD ME ACCOUNTABLE

Through his actions, Lee not only communicated what he expected from others but what others could expect of him. Lee had a personal drive to show his organization that what he said he would do would be done.

Rigor, responsibility and follow-through define Lee's style. He consistently applies this operating principle in business activities. It is most visible in the monthly performance measurement, reporting system, and leadership meeting. Lee ends every meeting with an action item list that outlines the subject, the task, the person responsible and the due date. Lee and the other officers conduct periodic checks to ensure that committed-to items are completed in a timely manner.

RELENTLESSLY PURSUE EXCELLENCE

The best example of Lee's optimistic, affirming approach was with four simple words that applied not only to the organization, but to each individual employee – "best of the best." These words gave a whole new meaning and served as the foundation for the new CL&P's vision, mission, values, and expectations. The recurring question that stemmed from these four words was, "Why not be the best?"

Striving to be the best can sound like nothing more than motivational rhetoric; therefore, one of Lee's priorities was to be specific. To illustrate the level of performance indicative of a best-of-best company, the 2003 "In Focus" included a "benchmark box" for each key result area that compared CL&P's 2002 performance with the best in the industry. Although CL&P can show considerable improvement, the ultimate goal, being the best, remains unchanged.

PERFORMANCE ENHANCEMENT SYSTEM (PES)

With his new officer team, Lee created the key result areas in a balanced scorecard manner and then identified the key performance indicators (KPI) required to measure each result area.

Subsequently, the team formalized the definition of each KPI and assigned an owner. Each owner took his KPI and created a basis document outlining the specifics. This included why the KPI is important, what it tells you when you measure it, and how it is calculated. The basis document also set the expected target level. These documents became the foundation for a new performance measurement process, which CL&P calls the Performance Enhancement System (PES). It started on a basic spreadsheet, and has grown into its own software application.

The PES process and system became one of Lee's critical management tools to define stakeholder requirements, communicate expectations, monitor results, and build a culture of accountability. It provided the answers to where we are trying to take this company, what key measures are needed to get there, what key initiatives need to be put in place, and what our priorities will be.

One director explained the learning process associated with PES. "Culturally, it took time to evolve. Lee was open to people telling him about the measurements, and why they may believe a KPI was not the right one. He empowered the owners to take their assigned KPI. We were given the opportunity to fix the data or create what it should be. The measures 'shook themselves out,' and dialogue occurred in monthly leadership meetings."

Once the measures were established, targets were finalized and KPI owners were held accountable to ensure that target performance levels were achieved or exceeded. Because Lee understands that striving for excellence is a never-ending process, new targets are set at the end of each year that further raise the bar.

The bar has been raised considerably during Lee's first two years at CL&P. The improvement as measured by PES shows that overall the organization is currently exceeding the established targets. Specific examples include improved safety with a 30-percent decrease in lost-time/restricted duty accidents, attaining 91-percent accuracy in projecting restoration times for customer outages versus a 51-percent starting point, and a 7-percent reduction in operating and maintenance costs per customer served.

3. Ask employees to tackle problems – you'll be amazed by the growth that results

When Lee took the leadership helm at CL&P, he was impressed with the level of experience and raw talent he observed among the 2,300 employees. He rightfully believed that if he provided the employees with the necessary tools and asked them to strive for excellence, they would be up to the challenge. Consistent with his belief in the power of the individual, Lee began a process to take decision-making and pride of ownership to the front-line level of the company.

BRING FORWARD THE BEST FROM THE PAST AND THEN LET GO

Instead of criticizing the organization he walked into, Lee often said, "This is a good company; my goal is to make it an excellent one." A disparaging comment toward other departments or past leadership was often intercepted by Lee, who turned it around with a question or statement focusing on what could be taken from the past toward achieving Lee's vision of a "best of the best" future for CL&P.

He considers the supervisor role as the most important one to achieving performance goals and acting as role models for change. Therefore, he felt the supervisor position and their issues must be given primary consideration in changing the culture. When planning his annual meeting with the organization's top 300 leaders, he empowered a cross-functional, multi-level employee design team to plan and execute the meeting. Half of the team was comprised of front-line supervisors and Lee asked them to make certain the issues of greatest interest to their constituents were addressed. A post-event assessment showed the vast majority of attendees clearly understood CL&P's direction and priorities, felt the company was heading in the right direction, and had an increased confidence in the company's ability to achieve that vision.

MAXIMIZE POTENTIAL

While some leaders prefer to tell the truth or realities of an organization with negative energy, Lee would often point out, "We need to learn to block out the negative thoughts and replace them with positive affirmations." He not only prescribed to providing individuals with experiences that allowed them to envision the possibilities, he

involved them in a journey of self-discovery with individual accountability for problem solving.

He ignited the future perspective, and consequently positive energy,
when he launched the *Imagine 21*™ program to all employees and the
Leadership Academy to all levels of supervision. Both of these interventions engaged the employees in self-discovery, practicing new
learning, setting goals, and being accountable for the desired future.

While respecting the past, Lee encouraged people to challenge the
status quo. He did this in a positive, visionary way to help the organization embrace change. By building the capacity to change throughout the organization, CL&P is becoming a more resilient, forward-
thinking culture.

INCREASE EMPLOYEE INVOLVEMENT
Having tapped into the power of individual contributors, Lee wanted
to instill a sense of ownership by involving all levels of employees in
the decision-making process. He felt to enhance creativity and innovation, leaders need to give people the power to initiate and sustain
efforts that seek their input and quick execution.

His commitment to employee input and his understanding of the
"real" organization's realities has been evident with the launching
of an employee advisory group that meets with him monthly, curriculum advisory boards that provide counsel on training needs, and
the inclusion of all employee levels (including union leadership) in
process improvement initiatives.

With Lee's leadership, CL&P adopted the WorkOut model pioneered
by General Electric. The WorkOut model brings together a team of
people from across the company, provides them with a challenge,
asks them to totally immerse themselves in generating solutions,
makes on-the-spot decisions during a "town meeting," and charges

the team with implementing the approved recommendations within a short (usually 90-day) timeframe.

The process is consistent with Lee's core belief in the power of the individual. He believes that those closest to the work will come up with far better solutions than leadership could create in a vacuum. Additionally, by asking people to make and implement recommendations, you are not only building efficacy, but also teaching them to be option thinkers and helping them to act like "owners," thereby enhancing morale.

The WorkOut model also teaches team members a participative approach to problem solving. The proof is in the results. For nearly eleven years, various teams had explored the opportunity of consolidating CL&P's three dispatch centers. Lee asked a team to tackle the issue and the results were astounding. In one year, they were able to plan and implement the consolidation into a single, state-of-the-art center. The project came in under budget and employees were impressed by the speed and effectiveness of this employee-led accomplishment. One employee said, "I would have never imagined that we would actually go to a single system's operation center." Another said, "We have gotten more done in the last six months than in years."

4. Affirm other people – it renews pride and builds a sense of accomplishment

As Lee has said on numerous occasions, "Our people are the foundation of this company." That philosophy guided virtually every action in his inside-out approach to transforming CL&P to a best-of-best company. It is the people who are the heart, soul and face of the company. Therefore, using the power of affirmations to instill confidence and pride becomes an essential behavioral characteristic in highly efficacious companies.

TREAT ALL WITH DIGNITY AND RESPECT

Regardless of whether he was designing the organizational structure, working on the selection and exit processes or weathering major resistance, Lee stressed the need to treat each individual with dignity and respect. This principle was tested many times during the first 90 days as he described the current realities and his vision for change with the previous senior team still in place. Because of the respect demonstrated, several officers provided Lee with critical business information.

HAVE A BIAS FOR RESULTS

In today's CL&P, the previously highlighted PES system is the means for monitoring progress and measuring results. To compensate people based on the results they achieve, bonuses are directly tied to attaining or exceeding the target performance level on those KPIs that are determined to have the greatest impact on the company, its people and its customers. To link individual to corporate-level performance wherever possible, KPIs are measured at the department/work center level and then aggregated for an overall CL&P score.

This level of measurement has led to friendly competition between locations and departments across the company. As each group strives for bragging rights, a renewed sense of teamwork has resulted. As one manager described this change, "Today, there is more of a focus on results. In the past what mattered was working real hard. Now there is a focus on delivering the results. What matters is delivering – not just trying."

CELEBRATE ACHIEVEMENTS

While Lee's operating style keeps a keen eye on the desired future state, he realizes how important it is to commemorate progress along the journey. These celebrations take many forms, ranging from large-group events to individual-level awards. To convey senior management's appreciation, Lee is personally involved on many of these occasions.

Lee arranged his schedule to kick off and end nearly every offering of the Leadership Academy. When field locations achieved safety milestones, Lee authorized celebratory breakfasts. To commemorate three area work centers attaining ISO 14001 certification, he arranged and attended luncheons. Realizing he could not personally participate in every event, he chose to lead by example and hoped other members of the leadership team would follow suit. They did. As the implementation of the WorkOut recommendations were completed, the officer sponsor would arrange an event to commemorate the breakthrough results that had been achieved. Care was taken to identify appropriate, moderately priced gift items that could be awarded to team members.

A SYSTEMATIC APPROACH TO CONTINUE THE TRANSFORMATION

CL&P's OPERATING MODEL

Lee realized he needed a model that communicated his integrated approach to business, and a set of mechanisms to institutionalize focus, alignment and accountability. The CL&P's model (See Table One) is an adaptation from Larry Bossidy's and Ram Charan's book, *Execution.*

While large group events are a great deal of fun and receive a good amount of attention throughout the organization, it is the more personal recognitions that epitomize Lee's valuing of individuals. He often takes the time to write a personal note of thanks to individuals who go above and beyond to deliver outstanding results. These "Lee notes" have become sought-after, prized rewards.

This integrated business model illustrates Lee's balanced priority and focus around CL&P's core processes of People, Strategy and

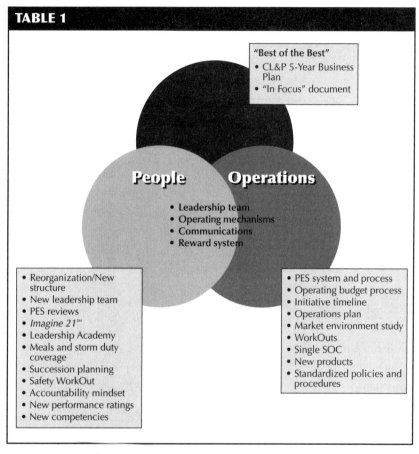

TABLE 1

"Best of the Best"
- CL&P 5-Year Business Plan
- "In Focus" document

People

Operations

- Leadership team
- Operating mechanisms
- Communications
- Reward system

- Reorganization/New structure
- New leadership team
- PES reviews
- *Imagine 21*™
- Leadership Academy
- Meals and storm duty coverage
- Succession planning
- Safety WorkOut
- Accountability mindset
- New performance ratings
- New competencies

- PES system and process
- Operating budget process
- Initiative timeline
- Operations plan
- Market environment study
- WorkOuts
- Single SOC
- New products
- Standardized policies and procedures

Operations. It also captures his belief that the glue to hold these processes together will be CL&P's leadership team, the communications, its reward system and operating mechanisms.

OPERATING MECHANISMS

A set of integrative mechanisms involving CL&P's leadership was created. These mechanisms were designed to build alignment, enhance working relationships, foster new ideas, build strategies, and foster new business and leadership concepts. They also served as forums

TABLE 2

Mechanism	Executive In-Focus Forum (EIFF)	In-Focus Forum (IFF)	EIFF 1 Strategy Review	EIFF 2 Operating Plan Review	PEOPLE Leadership Session	Annual Success Meeting
Meeting Owner	Lee Olivier, President	Lee Olivier, President	Lee Olivier, President	Lee Olivier, President	Lee Olivier, President	Lee Olivier, President
Length	1 Day	1 Day	1 Day	1 Day	1 Day	1 Day
Calendar	Bi-Monthly	Bi-Monthly	Annual - April	Annual - Oct.	Annual - Nov.	Annual - Dec.
Participants	President, Direct Reports, HR, VP-Utility Group Services, Communications	President, Direct Reports, Division Mgrs, Directors, HR, Communications, VP-Utility Group Services	President, Direct Reports, HR, VP-Utility Group Services, Communications	President, Direct Reports, HR, VP-Utility Group Services, Communications	President, Direct Reports, HR, VP-Utility Group Services, Communications, Org. Change & Learning (OCL)	President, Direct Reports, Division Mgrs, Managers, Directors, Communications, HR, VP-Utility Group Services, Org. Change & Learning (OCL)
Purpose	• Review all aspects of their business and external environment • Identify company's greatest opportunities and problems • Shape Best Practices • Observe how leaders think, work together and coach them • Strategy	• Leadership alignment on goals • Operationalizing new behaviors • Performance enhancement system reviews • Communication	• Discuss strategy for next 3 years • Discuss forward financial goals for Management Committee (MC) • Evaluate effectiveness of current strategies • Discuss external environment • Output CL&P's strategies for the next 3 years to be submitted for May's MC in prep. for July Board of Director mtg.	• Links CL&P strategies to operational priorities and resource allocation • Discuss operational plans (3-5 years)	• Leadership and organizational review • Organizational effectiveness priorities • Leadership development, strategies and plan • Culture change initiatives	• Management alignment annual meeting • Review current year's initiatives • Kick-off of operating plans for next year • Kick-off of next year's CL&P goals

where strategy, operations, and people owners provided status reports and corrective action plans on their initiatives and key performance indicators. (See Table Two)

FIVE-YEAR BUSINESS PLAN

The new operating model was first used and put to the test during the development of another milestone, a Five-Year Strategic Business Plan. In August 2002 at a leadership off-site forum, the issue of needing a CL&P strategic planning was identified. The group broke into cross-functional teams and developed the overall strategic plan, the operational plans, benchmarking and key stakeholder plans.

The plan laid out a targeted path, which will move CL&P toward being the "best of the best" of distribution utilities. Beyond the development of strategies, this effort produced additional alignment and learning while participating in the process.

SO WHAT HAS CHANGED?

The mindset has changed at CL&P. The people now see the visions of two years ago becoming a reality. They have been involved in new experiences and created their own contexts and reasons for change. They see accountability in action as results are soaring. The *Imagine 21*™ experience provided them the opportunity to see new horizons that many never envisioned as future possibilities.

The essence of the change is best captured with the following employee quotes.

"If someone told me two years ago that CL&P would look and act like it does today, I would have never believed it."

"CL&P is now being run like a business."

"They are doing what they said they would."

THE JOURNEY CONTINUES

As 2002 was the year of vision and transformational change, the focus of 2003 was using the new tools and capabilities in "delivering results." The *Imagine 21*™ program continues to contribute to the positive changes occurring at CL&P.

There is no doubt that considerable progress has been made on CL&P's journey to being a best-of-best business. Today's CL&P is more agile, results-driven and forward looking. By starting the transformation from the inside out, Lee is providing systematic leadership that builds on the successes to date.

During his first year at the helm, Lee's emphasis was on building capabilities and putting systems in place that would enable the company to achieve unprecedented results. Those systems included the PES system that established performance benchmarks and identified performance gaps. Work Management is CL&P's system for managing the workload. It encompasses a scheduling tool that provides a common software platform upon which CL&P can manage construction and design activities. As part of the implementation of this software platform, formal processes have been developed and documented to help CL&P execute work more effectively. Completion of "critical" maintenance has quadrupled under the new system.

The WorkOut process empowered teams and led to unprecedented option thinking. For example, the WorkOut team, challenged with addressing the installation of re-closing devices to automatically restore service to customers in areas where the technology was employed, came up with a process to install twice as many devices with the same amount of activity. The team's recommendations reduced capital expenditures by $27 million and customers are benefiting from shorter service interruptions due to the rapid proliferation of the technology across CL&P's service territory.

Leveraging the platforms put in place to close performance gaps became the focus of year two. The people of CL&P have embraced that challenge by delivering unprecedented results. Although the target goals were raised for 2003, to date 75 percent of all KPIs are at the target level or higher, with 47 percent at the "stretch goal" level. The leadership team is managing the company to deliver results that are beneficial for both the company's shareholders and customers. Productivity improvements have allowed the company to reach earnings targets. Customers are seeing benefits from increased investment in the electrical infrastructure that led to improved reliability. Notwithstanding weather, the average minutes that electrical service to a customer is interrupted in a year decreased by more than 40 percent from 2002 to 2003, and when the effect of the August 2003 blackout is subtracted, the length of interruptions is reduced to an impressive 70 percent.

We fully expect the benefits to CL&P customers will grow over the next few years. Now that the internal systems are in place and the company is successfully closing performance gaps, we can turn our full attention to the customers. The challenge for 2004 and beyond is for the company to firmly embed itself into the customers' value chain.

CL&P has served Connecticut for more than a century. Under Lee Olivier's leadership, it is building its internal capabilities and positioning itself to meet the ever-changing and increasingly sophisticated demands of its customers. It is transforming itself and is now well-positioned to fully meet the promise of its tagline by delivering "Energy for a changing world."

CREATING A *Thriving Culture*
SETTING THE PACE IN PERFORMANCE

By David Sabey, CEO
Sabey Corporation

GOALS, AFFIRMATIONS AND AN ACTION PLAN

As I get older, I am only more awed by the positive ways the teachings of The Pacific Institute have helped me both professionally and personally. A little background can help illustrate the enormity of my transformation.

Formal education wasn't a big deal in my family. My mother's schooling was cut short at the seventh grade because her dad died. At fourteen, she became the sole provider for her family. My dad's formal education ended with a high school diploma, which was fairly typical for those raised in The Depression. I didn't believe I was poor. We just didn't have anything. But my parents were the best. We didn't have much as far as physical possessions, but life was good for me and I grew up a very happy young boy.

My parents' goals for me were always modest. They told me, "Be a mailman" or "Work for the railroad." Those jobs were steady and they meant a regular paycheck. That was extremely important to my parents.

As such, I never had much academic pressure from them. I wasn't a bad student, though I think I could have been a much better student if my priorities had been different.

I was always big for my age, so playing sports was natural for me. Since my mom never drove a car, I always walked or rode my bike to school. In fact, I walked or rode my bike everywhere. Part of my success in sports, I think, can be attributed to the fact that all that bike riding as a kid certainly strengthened my legs and endurance.

My mom was never very comfortable with contact sports. She frequently lectured me, "We did without so that you would have a healthy body. Now look at you, all beat up. Why do you do this to yourself?"

In junior high, I did well in both football and track, and I met Mr. Tice. I guess it is still a bit unnatural for me to call Lou anything but Mr. Tice. Even though Lou and Diane have become great family friends, I will always think of them as teachers and mentors, not only for myself, but also to my family and the Sabey Corporation.

Back in the early sixties, Lou cruised the junior high feeder schools to Highline High School, to check out his "farm team." It was on one of these trips that I first met Lou. I knew it was a big moment for me when Coach Tice came over to my locker that day after practice. But I had no idea of how important that meeting would eventually turn out to be for me.

Two years later at Highline, Lou gave me two tools that have made all the difference in my life. First, he made all of us on the football team keep a personal notebook. We had to write down our goals for the year, the personal reason for these goals and we had to put together a clearly defined plan to make sure these goals were accomplished. We had to have goals, we had to have affirmations and we had to have an action plan. Goals, affirmations and an action plan – simple concepts, but very powerful concepts at the same time.

Second, Lou asked us to reject every excuse that held us back. He told us to go out and "dream the wildest dreams" and then we had to make that our goal. It was a powerful concept for me. What a set of gifts!

It may sound overly simplistic but success was immediate for me. During my senior year, I had four full-ride athletic scholarships to Dartmouth, US Air Force Academy, University of Washington and Washington State University. And it's been that way ever since. Goals, affirmations, action plans. And success.

I have had plenty of setbacks, but I've also been able to endure and ultimately succeed because of the tools I originally received from Mr. Tice, and then later from The Pacific Institute. They have taught me simple themes, and these themes have bound my life together.

Since then, I've had many other accomplishments, particularly with my company, the Sabey Corporation. They demonstrate how The Pacific Institute can help people break their own self-imposed boundaries. This allows them to set their own goals and achieve them. In many ways, I am an example of that.

As people, we are truly one big community. We're born in different places. We have different beginnings. We have all kinds of different experiences. But when you shake all that down, we have similar hardware. We all have opportunities. We all have certain basic skills. I call it our very own personal "software." Our "software" restricts or opens opportunities for us. If we learn to reprogram our software, we break the code and eliminate the restrictions. So, in reality, we're all in the business of "software reprogramming." We all have an obligation to break the code, to break out of our restrictions and continuously upgrade our personal software.

We also have to instill performance. Leadership is all about setting an example and then taking it one step further. We take the good out of what we've learned through our life's journey and we share it with as many people as we can. The Pacific Institute and Lou Tice teach us these codes that allow us to reprogram our personal software. We then can make decisions on what to do with our lives.

MOVE TOWARD AND BECOME LIKE THAT WHICH YOU THINK ABOUT

I'm a businessman. As the president and CEO of the Sabey Corporation, I've watched our company go through so much and I'm proud of all our accomplishments. Many of them illustrate how important leadership is and what is necessary to move people forward to accomplish great things. It's a familiar Pacific Institute theme and one that Lou Tice instilled in me years ago.

> *"It's important to move toward and become like that which you think about."*

There are many great examples of how The Pacific Institute and Tice's code have helped me, and the Sabey Corporation, move toward great goals and succeed. For example, Sabey Corporation has had a great list of clients and a great list of projects. We recently built a million-square-foot facility that we designed, engineered and own. Right now, an online news organization is served out of that facility. A major software company is served out of that facility. And a major international retailer's Internet is served through that facility.

Inside, there's lots of "gee whiz" stuff such as two rooms full of locomotive engines that are two-megawatt generators – seven engines each. We can generate enough power for a small city. We will eventually have six rooms of these generators in one building.

We also have data centers around the country and the world. We've built shopping centers. We even built a textile company. We were the largest supplier to Wal-Mart and Target. We rode Wal-Mart from 200 stores to 2,500 stores. We've won "Vendor of Excellence" awards from both of those companies.

I bought the hospital where I was born from the Sisters of Providence, a very fine organization that changed the world in many ways. The Sisters had to sell the facility because healthcare has these enormous cost pressures. They'd owned it for a hundred years and I said, "Well, I'm a good Catholic boy, I will take really good care of the Sisters' work," and every time the Sisters come around I start sweating. But it's turned into a great project.

Other Sabey projects include the regional facility for the Department of Homeland Security in Tukwila and a defense facility in Tucson. We've done a lot of work for the military. We're building these facilities and we're building them well. Actually, we're not only doing it well, we're doing it the best. We are really good at what we do.

This journey I've been on has been awesome. I've made money and I've lost money. Fortunately, I've made a lot more than I've lost. And in the process, I've done a lot of exciting things. But, the tools of The Pacific Institute help on both sides of the equation.

Here's the other side of the equation. When I was 43, I lost millions in one deal. My wife said to me, "Don't ever do that again." But money doesn't mean much to me. It's important in one way, because no money, no mission. It takes juice to do big things. And there's nothing wrong with making money. It's what you do with it that's important. It's what you do with your time as a result. If you're successful, you have an obligation to give back.

But ultimately it isn't about the money. It's about the platform. It's about the credential it gives you to go do great things. And that's what matters to me, doing great things. I believe my vocation in life is to help create family-wage jobs, high paying jobs so people can support themselves with dignity. It's the philosophy of giving a man a fish and you give him a meal. But if you teach him how to fish, he can feed himself.

Human beings are all about evolving – being all they can be. The Pacific Institute helps people do that. They say, "Stop listening to everybody else and start thinking for yourself." Thinking is the key word.

We all have to start thinking about who we are, who we want to be and what we can do. There are no more excuses if we set goals. It's not easy. There's got to be tenacity and hard work. But it can be done. And we should have good, fun projects that we're proud to be part of.

One such project we had fun with is the 1990 Goodwill Games, which was originally an idea of Ted Turner's. Ted Turner created CNN and changed the world in a number of ways by connecting people and getting information out. Ted Turner came to Seattle and he wanted to do something. He had a mission, the Goodwill Games. What I liked about the Goodwill Games was that it involved two Pacific Institute themes. One, the Goodwill Games allowed us to send a positive picture of the Pacific Northwest to the rest of the world. Second, it went back to the idea of "moving toward and becoming like what you think about."

At first, there was a lot of controversy in the Pacific Northwest when Ted Turner came with this idea. This was a deal with the Russians when the Russians weren't exactly our best friends.

It's amazing how people spend an enormous amount of time thinking about what they can't do as opposed to what they can do. The Goodwill Games allowed us to help change the way the community thought of itself. All of a sudden, we could do something that people didn't think we could do. We became a first class sports venue. We became a place where world records were set.

I remember one of my goals for the Goodwill Games was to build something for a world record event. So I got involved with getting the Goodwill Games pool built. But it cost 23 million bucks. Instead of just sitting and waiting for money to roll in, we raised the money ourselves. Then we designed and built it. Megan Quann now has two gold medals. And we have world records set in our pool.

WHO DO YOU SURROUND YOURSELF WITH?

This spring, I was on the base camp at Mount Everest with my good friend Jim Whittaker and Sir Edmund Hillary. Whittaker was the first American on Everest and Hillary was the first man to conquer it. Here's a key Pacific Institute question, "Who do you surround yourself with?" I don't think I'm doing too badly.

The point is, who is giving you great advice? Who is providing you with key input? Are you with colleagues who aren't making it? Or are you with people who have done great things? Whittaker and Hillary – these are great men. Whittaker is 73 years old, and he motored right up the mountain. When we got to the top, there were all these doctors testing heart rates and oxygen saturation. There's not much oxygen up there and the human body doesn't like it. But Whittaker's oxygen saturation is 76, which is pretty good.

When the doctors tested me, I'm at 70 percent saturation, which is kind of low. Whittaker says, "Why don't you try this pressure breathing?" I replied, "Geez, Whittaker, thank you for telling me about pressure breathing now that I'm already up here."

It's the perfect illustration of how many times we go through life and somebody tells you the solution to a problem after we've solved it ourselves.

The real question is, how many great solutions can you find to life issues and act on them?

You move toward and you become like that which you think about. Those are simple words, but the irony is what The Pacific Institute teaches is pretty simple. It's common sense. It's the way we work. What Lou has done is develop a great way to simplify a process that the world loves to complicate. He has simplified it so that we can all understand it and we can all adopt it. We have this enormous capacity within ourselves to do great things. We need to get beyond people who tell us we can't.

We all have our early history. But mine would never have indicated, in my view, where I am today if you went back and said, "Who is this guy and what's he likely to be?" I'd have been really good at what I did. I would probably be a really good gas station attendant, or I'd probably be a really good postman, and those are very fine jobs. Perhaps I could have been a lot of fine things. But then Lou came along and changed my whole view in life about what I could be.

There are lots of people who broke the code. There was Rene Descartes and "Cogito ergo sum - I think, therefore I am." Look back in history and you'll find people were thinking about these same things. There was Goethe who said, "Until one is committed, there is hesitancy."

As leaders, we need to tell our people we **can** instead of we can't.

As leaders, do we energize our people? If we're going to sustain performance or grow performance within our organizations, we've got to energize our own people to buy into our vision of what the mission is. We energize them by showing what we can do.

As leaders, we also have to stand up for what we believe in. Do we have a moral compass? Do we have a compass that helps us sort out what's garbage and keep what's good?

And as leaders, we must have a picture of what we hope to accomplish and then execute it. Nothing gets accomplished if we sit around and talk about a project but nobody does anything about it. It's not enough just to talk about the code and changing the software. We have to get it done, and we have to keep **using** the code and constantly upgrading it.

You know what happens if you're a runner and you stop for a couple months? It's tough to get going again. It hurts. You have to keep going. You have to keep working. You have to keep learning. It isn't about sustaining performance; it's about using each block to build yourself higher. How high can you go? What is the limit?

I've had a very lucky life. When I was a kid, I had a poster of Eugene "Big Daddy" Lipscomb on my wall, and every night, at 11 years old, I prayed to be just like Big Daddy Lipscomb, a defensive end for the Baltimore Colts. I said "I want to be six-foot-six and 265 pounds," every night. But then I met Lou Tice, and my life was indelibly changed.

My mom, who I love and is my hero, has said to me through the years: "Dave, why are you doing sports? We did without so you would be healthy. Dave, why are you in this construction business? Get out of that construction business. Be a postman or a railroad guy – he gets a regular paycheck. Why aren't you getting a job like that? Dave, who cares about education? What the heck do those guys know?"

I love my mom and I respect her. We all can identify with questions like that, and we all have people telling us stuff that might hold us back.

Whatever you can do, or dream you can do, begin it. Boldness has genius, power and magic. We have this enormous capacity within ourselves to do great things. Who and what is programming your software? What are you thinking about right now? Who do you listen to?

I learned a basic truth from Lou Tice when I was just a kid, and I broke the code. I've moved toward and became what I thought about. And as Lou would tell you as well, this basic truth has evolved, and it continues to evolve.

Guys like me are soldiers of the Institute and testimonies for what you can do. I don't know what I would have been without it, but I know what I am and what I've done. And I don't care about what I've done, because I don't think much about the past. What I think about, what sparks me up, what pegs my fun meter, is what are we going to do in the future?

Caterpillar
Employee Engagement and Satisfaction

By Ernest Skipper
Caterpillar Logistics (USA and UK)

First, I shall describe some of my experiences in applying the concepts of The Pacific Institute (TPI) to a number of responsibilities I have had in my thirty plus years with Caterpillar.

Then I shall tell you about the achievement of what we called the Bold Goal approach in the identification of goals, the development of an organizational structure and an implementation plan, all designed to accelerate the accomplishment of goals. Special emphasis will be given to the importance of employee satisfaction, or employee engagement, in the accomplishment of organizational goals.

The General Manager of the Lafayette facility of Caterpillar asked me to take on the job of Employee Assistance Representative, which was to deal with problems raised by employees who couldn't get resolution with their managers. We were having some issues around empowerment. Basically, it came down to the fact that people had learned the vocabulary, but they just weren't walking the talk. I was asked to find potential training programs that would align the actions with the words.

I went to Seattle to take part in The Pacific Institute's program, *Investment in Excellence*® *(IIE),* and was convinced that this program had useful applications for our business. I then convinced management to roll it out to all the employees in the Lafayette facility. Strangely, despite being convinced the program would work for us, I did not take it on board immediately. The reason for that is the first time I attended *IIE* I didn't get as much out of it personally because I was evaluating it for other people. It was only when we had facilitators come to Lafayette, and I looked at the material again with a focus on what I could get out of it that I became totally convinced that it was just what I needed. I began to explore my inner thoughts and beliefs, and found some of the things that were holding me back. After some reflection, I realized that what was holding me back had nothing to do with Caterpillar or anybody else. I was holding me back.

When I began to implement the concepts of the program, things began to shift very quickly. It has been an amazing ride. I've had opportunities I never even dreamed about before. In the past, I was always looking for somebody's approval, and when things went wrong, I was always looking for someone else to blame. I looked for the negative in most situations, and not surprisingly, I often found it. I had a quick temper in stressful situations, and I also had a belief that I had very little influence from where I was in the organization.

I began to develop the affirmations to work on changing those beliefs. It was only three months later that I was made training manager and had the chance to develop a new strategy to move things along.

My new approach, attitude and performance, began to be noticed in the organization. I was offered the opportunity to set up and manage the Inbound Logistics Center in Champaign, Illinois. I came close to declining the offer. I liked the role I was in, and was very comfortable with it. It was only with some encouragement from my manager and the realization that I would have more opportunity to influence the overall change within Caterpillar from Champaign that I accepted the offer.

Using the concepts learned in *Investment in Excellence*®, I began facilitating the development of a vision with the new management team. We established some difficult targets for getting the facility up and running. We didn't just want to have it done on time and on budget. We wanted to have it functioning so well that our customer contacts would come to see what we were doing differently causing such a big change from the previous service provider.

Steve Wunning, then president of Cat Logistics, saw the implementation as an incredible success. We had succeeded in getting the facility in operation on schedule and on budget, without letting any of the usual problems affect the implementation. It turned out to be a significant accomplishment that met client requirements from day one. Clients started dropping in to see what was being done so differently at the facility.

We worked with The Pacific Institute in getting all facility employees through the *Investment in Excellence* program. Then came another offer to become the Vice President of Human Resources for Cat Logistics. Again, I saw this offer as another opportunity to have a stronger influence in the organization, another position that would enable me to have an influence in creating the Caterpillar I believed we could be.

The management team in Champaign followed through with the plan that had been established, and the implementation was a tremendous success. The Inbound Logistics Center looked at several measures of the impact of the program throughout the course of the implementation. A large majority of the employees surveyed rated the program as effective or very effective at helping them to manage stress and interact more smoothly with others.

Looking back on it, I thought this might be the end of the road for my career, that things could not be much better than this. However, it was not long before I realized that this was just a stepping-stone for other opportunities.

My next move took me well out of my comfort zone, thousands of miles geographically, and no small distance culturally, to Leicester, England. Again, I turned to The Pacific Institute.

A few months after accepting the new assignment, Cat Logistics succeeded in renewing and expanding a 10-year contract with the BMW Group to supply warehousing and third party logistics for Rover and Land Rover. The scope of the contract was much larger than before, and the challenge was to increase the site's capacity to handle the demands of the new contract with BMW due to start in 2002. Before then, the Leicester facility had to reconfigure its existing warehouse, more than double its warehouse space to over a million square feet, and expand personnel by 90 percent, while not sacrificing the quality of service our clients were accustomed to having.

This was a real challenge. The Leicester team's assessment of the current reality was quite stark. Operations manager, Steve Battle summed it up simply: We came to the conclusion that if we carried on doing what we had been doing, we were going to have some problems. We then turned again to The Pacific Institute. According to Battle, one of the main goals of engaging The Pacific Institute was to assist us in creating a new culture for the company prior to recruiting new staff members. To quote Battle, "We want to create a better culture, a better environment, and a better way of doing things, so that people really want to come to work. We would like to see everybody get involved in that, to have some fun, and to accomplish things at the same time."

The management team went through *IIE* in October and November of 1999, and followed up with a Communications Day and a Strategic Vision Building workshop in December 1999. It is important to note that the initiative was not rolled out in isolation, but as part of an integrated approach to capacity building that also included technical and systems training.

At the time, we had 315 employees, and about 14 months later, 250 more were to be added. All current staff were to experience the *IIE* program before then. We were firm in our belief that we needed to create a new culture before the new staff arrived. We wanted to put the new people through Phase 1 of the program before they got into the warehouse. We planned to tell them that this is how we do things here, and if they started work and did not see us using this material, they would have had a major disconnect.

I was quite impressed with the enthusiasm of our team. Of the 40 managers initially taken through the program, *Investment in Excellence®*, 22 volunteered to work as facilitators in the implementation. That same enthusiasm was also seen in the next layers to participate. Of the first 145 employees that went through *IIE*, 94% of them rated the program at a 4 or higher on a 5 point scale.

To further stress the importance of the concepts in *IIE* to their role in Caterpillar, we established a purpose-built resource center to enhance the sessions, promote our mission and values, and provide access to additional material and learning. We also produced a bi-monthly newsletter, "Self-Talk" to relay stories about individuals' personal and professional achievements with the concepts of *Investment in Excellence.*

With the change at Leicester on its way, I was offered a new position in the United States as Americas Manager for Caterpillar Distribution Services, in the newly formed Logistics Division within Caterpillar. The goals were preset for me to a large extent, and the bottom line was to radically change the way we did business. This division was viewed as having the best product support capabilities in the world, but at a cost that exceeded that of others in the industry. The challenge was to drastically reduce costs without reducing the service quality.

I decided to co-facilitate The Pacific Institute's curriculum to those reporting directly to me. I felt very comfortable with the idea of facilitating the program because of my experience in Leicester. By facilitating the program at this level, I wanted to support the personal development of each manager, helping them realize the benefits they would receive at their facility with a full roll-out of the program. It was gratifying to see the growth in most of the managers and to know from experience elsewhere that it will continue. Again, the results were dramatic. We exceeded the goal for 2000 by 148%!

The improvements are continuing. In the wake of the reorganization that created the new division, the main value drivers were defined, and for the operations division, warehouse productivity improvement was the main focus. We tracked each facility every month evaluating them in relation to their targets. All fifteen were quickly ahead of their glide path on the way to exceeding their ambitious year-end goals. One of them was 52% ahead, and several others were from 15 to 40% ahead of the goal at year-end 2001.

The use of The Pacific Institute's curriculum and Strategic Vision Building sessions has had an impact on our business. It is not the only factor, but it has been a big contributor to our success.

We also believe that our success is largely due to the dedication of our people. There will always be an emphasis on business success, but without the trust, confidence and support of our employees, we can't get to where we want to go. We are demonstrating that not only are we a world-class provider, but that we are the best there is in service and quality, at the lowest possible cost.

THE BOLD GOALS PROJECT

At the outset if this report, I indicated that the first part of this report would be directed toward the full scope of my use of The Pacific Institute's programs in my career with Caterpillar. This has been accomplished.

The second section of this report focuses on the "Bold Goals" program, an accelerated program designed to establish Cat Logistics as the best logistics company in the world – Lowest Cost, Highest Quality, Best Service. Special attention is given to the Bold Goals initiative, with emphasis on the value of employee satisfaction or employee engagement.

As referred to earlier, in early 2000, Caterpillar consolidated several units that performed logistics functions in various divisions into one group, Logistics Division, commonly called Cat Logistics. The purpose of this consolidation was to achieve synergies, thereby reducing costs and improving the quality of service to our customers. I was named Americas manager for the newly formed Caterpillar Distribution Services, within Cat Logistics. In this role, I was responsible for 15 facilities and 19 direct reports throughout the U.S., Canada, Mexico and Brazil.

I knew that the facilities had only averaged 3% productivity improvement per year for the past several years, and the Bold Goal was to achieve an improvement of 34% over the next three and one half years. A new belief in what would be possible was needed.

We organized a four-day meeting, spending the first two days taking all of my reports through The Pacific Institute's *Imagine 21*™ workshop. This approach, which I co-facilitated, built a personal bond with my reports and opened them to new possibilities, and a new way of thinking. The next two days were spent talking about the Bold Goals and what the Americas Distribution Services division would be like in three years, when it had become a part of the best logistics company in the world. At the end of the two-day vision session, a document was created stating in the present tense what it would be like at the end of 2003. Stated simply, affirmations of the desired future.

Four weeks later, the group came back together to complete the two-day *Imagine 21*™ Phase II workshop, and to finalize and achieve consensus on the vision document. At no time during these sessions were there any efforts made to develop a project plan. The immediate goal was to get everybody solidly locked onto the Bold Goals.

After returning to their facilities, each manager started facilitating discussions with their staff, and brainstorming process improvement ideas.

PROJECT APPROACH

Following the completion of the *Imagine 21* workshop, it was decided that I would personally facilitate a series of six more *Imagine 21* workshops for managers, supervisors and team leaders within the division, to insure consistency. Phase II of the workshops were tightly tied into a hierarchy of what we called "smart goals" to be achieved over the next three and one half years. The "smart goals" were balanced between:

a. Employee Satisfaction

b. Customer Satisfaction

c. Stockholder Satisfaction

The specific facility smart goals were established, using benchmark data. This insured that all facilities would improve to at least the top two sector quintiles, as determined by the benchmark data, in terms of quality (accuracy of stock in stores, number of shipping errors) and productivity (expressed in lines handled, LHY, per employee/year).

A monthly reporting process was developed and implemented at the end of the first month. This results-tracking process included a "Dashboard" report for each facility showing the progress being made against each goal. Also, an annual recognition process, previously used, was modified and tied directly to the balanced goal achievement for each facility. This process was referred to as the Caterpillar Excellence Award.

BEHAVIORAL CHANGES

The managers, indeed the whole organization became highly committed to the goals, and also improved its trust in leadership as evidenced by employee satisfaction surveys. This led directly to substantial operational improvements exceeding the ambitious Bold Goals. Specifically, each of the 15 facilities, and not just the ones most visible to senior management, delivered substantial improvements on an ongoing basis; relationships with the workforce and their union improved tangibly (improved employee satisfaction, fewer "high level" grievances).

OPERATIONAL RESULTS

By the end of the first 18 months, ending in December 2001, the Americas group had accomplished radical improvements as compared to the 1999 baseline.

a.   A 24% improvement in LHY productivity, leading to 178 fewer people in the organization – mostly through attrition, and not replaced.

b.   Total operating costs per line shipped reduced by 19.2%

c. Dealer claims reduced by 22.5%

d. New inventory accuracy performance record established

e. Many managers not previously identified as "high potential" were given new and expanded opportunities.

FINANCIAL RESULTS

The above operational results were estimated to represent an annual savings of several million dollars, with little or no capital expenditure. The implementation of *Imagine 21*™ was judged to have made a substantial contribution to the achievement of these results. This contribution can be estimated at about 25% of the total saving, by comparing the Americas groups' improvements (using *Imagine 21*) with the other groups' improvements that used the traditional project improvement process. The cost of the program was minimal, when compared to the actual savings achieved.

LESSONS LEARNED

a. Commitment from the top was essential. A senior manager's direct involvement and ongoing support were critical for success.

b. Clear and Bold Goals were set for the 20% of the areas which would yield 80% of the benefits, using a credible benchmark approach.

c. Focus was on securing strong commitment to the goals and to a clear vision, rather than on the formal project planning of "how to get there."

d. Consistent messages and common answers to questions contributed to the trust and commitment to the goals and vision.

RELATIONSHIP BETWEEN PRODUCTIVITY AND EMPLOYEE SATISFACTION

One interesting statistic was identified when comparing the 2001 productivity with the 2000 results. The five facilities with the lowest Employee Satisfaction scores only achieved an average productivity improvement of 13.2%, while the five facilities with the highest satisfaction achieved a 15% improvement. (These were already the higher productivity facilities.) One may say that there is not much difference between 13.2% and 15%. However, in this case, it is estimated that approximately $350,000 more would have been saved if every facility had achieved the higher level of performance.

The graph below demonstrates the relationship between productivity and employee satisfaction, most commonly referred to as employee engagement. The facilities are ordered by the lowest to the highest level of employee satisfaction. Satisfaction is plotted on the right

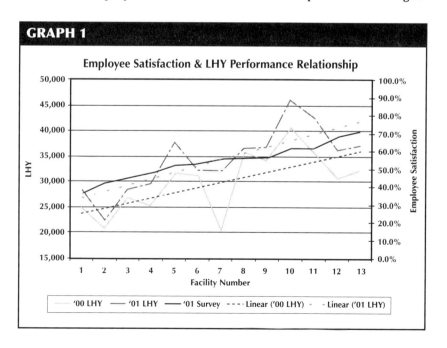

GRAPH 1

Employee Satisfaction & LHY Performance Relationship

axis, and productivity on the left axis. The linear regression line for the 2001 production is steeper than the one for 2000. This is a clear example of the power of employees when engaged – the higher the employee satisfaction, the higher the productivity, and the higher the productivity in 2000, the more improvement in 2001.

Is it true, the harder employees work, the more satisfied they are? Or is it the more engaged they are, the more productive they are? I think we all know the answer. We give much credit to TPIs implementation of *Imagine 21*™ for increasing our employees' engagement and productivity.

TEACHER AND PRINCIPAL
Self-Efficacy STUDIES

By Jeffrey J. Smith, Ed.D., Roger Freeman Ed.D. and Theresa Cole, M.Ed.

This chapter contains two distinct sections. Part I is a review of two recent studies conducted to measure the effectiveness of The Pacific Institute's program, 21 Keys for High Performance Teaching and Learning™. *Jeffrey J. Smith, Ed.D. and Roger Freeman, Ed.D., designed and administered two revealing studies measuring the change in perceived self- and collective efficacy of teachers and principals who attended the training. It is obvious that Bandura's Efficacy Theory is the conceptual basis of the study. In Part II, Theresa Cole presents supportive and qualitative items in the form of testimonials.*

PART I

In the first study, we explored the beliefs teachers hold about the self-efficacy of low performing students and high performing students, as well as their own self-efficacy beliefs. A sample group of 142 teachers from four schools from a large urban school district located in Phoenix, Arizona participated in this study. The teachers that were included ranged in grade levels from Kindergarten through 8th grade.

The second study recognized the varied success of schools in improving performance and asserted that the efficacy of the school leader, and the collective-efficacy of their colleagues, were factors in these variations. The study used a convenience sample of 68 principals and assistant principals from all grade levels with varied experience and school accountability profiles. Participants were from various regions of Arizona from workshops held between the spring of the 2003 and the fall of the 2004.

In each of these studies, identical survey items were administered before and after the seminar format treatment, creating repeated measures with an intervention design. Prior to participating in the *21 Keys for High Performance Teaching and Learning*™, participants were asked to respond to a questionnaire focused on their own personal perceptions of self-efficacy and those of the group with which they worked: students in the case of teachers, and teachers in the case of school leaders. Eleven survey items were used to assess the research questions for the teacher study. Eight survey items were used to assess the two research questions, which were focused on measuring changes in school leaders' beliefs.

Because a significant portion of these surveys included group-referent items, collective-efficacy concepts were examined. The belief of the group that it can execute an action or outcome – in this case, the faculty of a school – has the same four influences as self-efficacy: mastery experience, vicarious experience, verbal persuasion, and affective change. The group members share mutual inference, which is greater than the sum of each person's beliefs. Individuals with strong group affiliation are higher in collective-efficacy and those on the periphery have higher personal self-efficacy. Other researchers have found that high collective-efficacy is a stronger predictor of school performance than other aspects of the school context (race or socioeconomic status).

After treatment, teachers and school leaders were surveyed with the same questionnaires. Changes in these teachers' and school leaders' perceptions of themselves and their students or colleagues were analyzed by comparing the pre- and post-survey results. Each pair of questions illustrated a significant change from pre-test to post-test. While numerous tables were reported in these two studies, summaries of the results are reported in Figure 1, and Tables 1 and 2. Using a combined scale of the first five questions in the questionnaire, the teachers' perception of their self-efficacy was significantly different following a two-day focused in-service on self-efficacy.

Considerable support for the strong influence of *21 Keys* on judgments of self-efficacy was reinforced. The results of this study indicate that the *21 Keys,* video based, facilitated program was a highly effective approach to increasing the self-efficacy of teachers. This study also indicates that the perceptions teachers hold about their students can be positively influenced. The presence of a general treatment effect, across all research questions, provided strong evi-

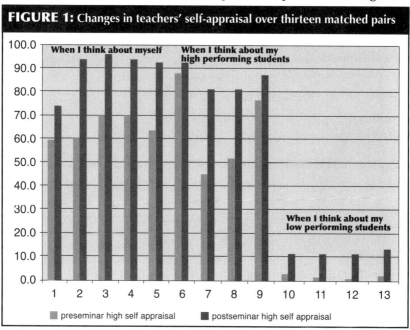

FIGURE 1: Changes in teachers' self-appraisal over thirteen matched pairs

dence that an increase in the self-efficacy of teachers was obtained through the *21 Keys* experience. Figure 1 shows the change in mean percentage of teachers indicating excellent or above average ratings for the thirteen items surveyed.

Teachers participating in the study also expressed growth on a personal level. End of seminar surveys reflect a high level of satisfaction in teachers. Examples of participant comments regarding the *21 Keys* experience include: *"Insightful, thought provoking and life changing," "I am a better parent knowing what I have learned in the past two days," "It gave me a new improved outlook," "The 21 Keys is life changing!" "Thanks for the opportunity to look into myself," "I am looking forward to my 30th year of teaching and not retirement."* From both quantitative and qualitative data, it is clear that the *21 Keys* video assimilation program with Lou Tice overwhelmingly affects people in the most positive ways.

For school leaders the survey items were combined into two referent groupings: self and collective referent. Research question one addressed the Personal Efficacy Construct or self-referent items, and question two addressed Collective-Efficacy Construct or colleague referent items. The mean ratings for school leaders' pre- and post-intervention judgments (5 representing *Excellent* and 1 being *Poor*) and paired sample t-test results are displayed in Tables 1 and 2.

The Personal Efficacy Construct Grouping was a series of four items sensing the building level school leaders' perceptions of their own self-confidence, their understanding of how their beliefs and thoughts determine their future, their knowledge of how to build self-confidence in themselves, and finally their attitudes toward setting goals in their schools. The personal efficacy construct grouping demonstrated a mean increase of 0.83 points on a 5-point Likert-type scale in the school leaders' perceptions of their own self-efficacy as measured by the survey instrument.

The change in the personal efficacy construct variable was significant with a mean increase in the percentage of *Excellent* or *Above
Average* self-perception by school leaders of 41.5%. The personal
efficacy construct grouping demonstrated a significant change in the
school leaders' perceptions of their own self-efficacy when questions
1 through 4 were combined into one variable to test the first research question. Table 1 shows that the personal efficacy construct
variable showed a significantly positive t-statistic. The aggregate
means of the school leaders indicated that they had *Above Average*
or *Excellent* level of self-referent efficacy of 55.1% before the intervention compared to 96.7% afterwards.

TABLE 1: School Leader's Self-Perceived Personal Efficacy Judgment	
Personal efficacy: Summary of means and significance of variance	
Pre-test	Post-test
3.60 $T(67) = 11.875$, p < .01	4.44

The collective-efficacy construct grouping was a series of four questions sensing the building level educational leaders' perceptions of
their teacher colleagues' self-confidence (as a group), their understanding of how their teacher colleagues' beliefs and thoughts determine their future, their knowledge of how to build self-confidence in
themselves, and finally their teacher colleagues' attitudes toward setting goals in their schools. The collective-efficacy construct grouping
demonstrated a mean increase of 0.70 points on a 5-point scale in the
school leaders' estimation of the self-efficacy and confidence of their
teacher colleagues as measured by the survey instrument.

The change in the collective-efficacy construct variable was significant with a mean increase in the percent of *Excellent* or *Above Average* self-perception by school leaders of 39.3%. The collective-efficacy

construct grouping demonstrated a significant change in the school leaders' estimation of the collective-efficacy and confidence of their teacher colleagues when questions 5-8 were combined into one variable to test the second research question. Table 2 shows that the collective-efficacy construct variable showed a significant positive t-statistic. The aggregate means of the school leaders indicated that they had *Above Average* or *Excellent* levels of self-referent efficacy of 32.4% before the intervention compared to 71.7% afterwards.

TABLE 2: School Leader's Self-Perceived Collective-Efficacy Judgment	
Collective efficacy: Summary of means and significance of variance	
Pre-test	Post-test
3.19 $T(67) = 8.932$, p < .01	3.89

Both of these research studies provide considerable support for the strong influence of a verbal persuasion model on judgments of self-efficacy, especially when accompanied by vicarious and mastery experiences as reinforcement. There were strongly significant positive statistics for each survey item and a significant positive difference in teachers and school leaders who participated in the structured intervention. The participants of these studies experienced a change in their level of self-confidence as evidenced by a significant difference following the *21 Keys* program. While some caution is appropriate in interpreting these findings, because of a relatively untested instrument, a convenience sample, minor delivery variations, and possible social effects, the strength of the statistical measures is persuasive. School leaders' perceptions of their personal self-efficacy and the collective-efficacy of their teacher colleagues were significantly different after participating in *21 Keys for High Performance Teaching and Learning*™.

Evidence suggests that high efficacy groups are characterized by being highly focused on obtainable goals, taking responsibility for outcomes, being highly collaborative, and changing more readily. We both recommend further study on long-term influences on school performance to help narrow the estimation of the limiting variables. It would be helpful to learn if the impact of *21 Keys* expanded to the collective-efficacy of the school unit that was under the leadership of principals who had participated in the seminar. One example might be the application of Goddard's collective-efficacy instrument (Goddard, 2000) in a post-hoc comparison of higher mean collective-efficacy schools and lower mean collective-efficacy schools to illuminate the differences in their implementation of *21 Keys* over a longer period.

PART II

This section represents ongoing anecdotal evidence of the effectiveness of The Pacific Institute's *21 Keys for High Performance Teaching and Learning* in focusing adult commitment on student learning, across a school district as a whole.

Education is a funny thing – it's not like business where there is a "bottom line" that can be objectively measured easily. Statistics don't quantify the look in a child's eye when they "get it" or measure the impact of the words a child hears every day. We do know that when a teacher exudes a belief in each student's ability to learn, children thrive; if a teacher believes, "there is no way," children flounder. In the face of difficulty, one teacher can drive a classroom toward antagonism and hostility, another toward optimism, even inspiration. Though often invisible or ignored entirely, this crucial aspect of teaching determines the effectiveness of everything else a teacher does.

21 Keys has opened opportunities for me to meet and work with educators across the United States over the past four years – exposing them to the concepts and supporting them in implementing those concepts. Throughout this work, I have reaped a rich harvest of anecdotal data from participants. Over and over, people attest that the pay-off of *21 Keys* has extended not only into their effectiveness in the classroom, but into their personal and family lives as well. One principal recently reported that she has lost 50 lbs., roughly an average-sized kindergartner. Participants commonly report these types of results. Using the information, they find themselves losing weight, paying off debt, enjoying their own children more, and improving their relationship with their spouse.

In my own school, my principal has credited *21 Keys* for helping launch a mindset shift and establish a performance culture among staff. The results speak for themselves. We have had a strong positive trajectory of passing rates on the Washington Assessment of Student Learning (WASL) for the last three years, and currently lead our district in all areas of the assessment at the middle school level. The questions inspired by *21 Keys* are not just, *"Are we doing what we need to do?"* but *"To what level are we doing what we need to do and where do we want to increase our efforts?"* The vast majority of teachers on our staff have developed a deep unwavering commitment to student learning. Teachers are taking personal accountability for successes and challenges, not only in their own classrooms but also in our effectiveness school wide. As a result, they are consciously abandoning activities in their classrooms that do not help students reach the targets and demonstrate mastery. My school, like many others that have implemented *21 Keys* as part of their school improvement plan, is undergoing sustained, continuous improvement.

There is no silver bullet in education; no plan or legislative bill that will inspire change in the way we do business with kids. *21 Keys* is a means to an end... not the end.

Implementing *21 Keys* fosters teaching that gets results. Following are just a few anecdotal results, unsolicited, that I have received from participants:

A PRINCIPAL WRITES:

Theresa: As I have shared with you before, yours was one of the best workshops I have participated in and the positives just continue to surface in my building. Over 60% of our 4-8 graders qualified for Honor Roll or High Honor Roll. We are experiencing about half of the misconduct referrals compared to last year. Recently, we were recognized as the best elementary school in the NW Phoenix suburban area. I believe that a lot of this is attributable to the information we have implemented from the *21 Keys* training. NOTE: My golf game has also improved greatly – to a zero handicap! — *January 2005*

AN ELEMENTARY TEACHER REPORTS:

Because of *21 Keys*, I realized that I need to be more aware of the pre-judgments I make about kids. I am now able to see kids where they are, and aim high from there. I now have more positive ways to approach kids and their parents. I see such differences every day. — *November 2004*

A SUPERINTENDENT EMAILS:

21 Keys is having an incredibly positive impact on our district. To date, we have trained 97% of all employees, including maintenance and support staff. After just a few months, we are already experiencing changes and creating a new culture of success. Thank you for all you have done to make this happen. — *November 2004*

After experiencing *21 Keys*, people have the tools to adopt an approach that frees the best in students and helps them to excel:

AN ELEMENTARY TEACHER SHARES:
When I took *21 Keys* I didn't know if I would be able to apply it. But I've found that I'm looking at all the kids differently, and it's making a huge difference in their attitudes. In the past, if a kid did something I didn't appreciate or think was right, I'd assume he or she just had a bad attitude. Now I am using what I learned in *21 Keys* way more than I ever thought I would. It's very powerful. It's making a big difference. — *January 2005*

A PRINCIPAL WRITES:
I've been dealing with three particularly challenging parents the last couple of days. Their kids have gotten themselves into quite a bit of trouble. As parents, they are frustrated, angry and aren't able to get past that sometimes. I have been saying to them, with genuine belief, things like, "I see Joe as being a kind-hearted, capable boy who makes good decisions; in this instance, he made a poor choice. That's not like him. Joe is a good kid who is full of potential. Let's move on, to get to that potential." Sometimes, parents need people to affirm the goodness in their children. It's invaluable to them to know that school "authority figures" see worth and goodness in their children. It changes their approach when dealing with their kids when they have done something out of line. *21 Keys* applies in so many ways, and I wanted you to know. — *October 2004*

AN ELEMENTARY TEACHER SAYS:
I have a child in my classroom who started off the year telling me that he couldn't do what I was teaching. He would look at his work, shake his head, and come to tell me that he was "no good" in math. I started using the techniques from *21 Keys*. At first, the changes started slowly; now he notices his successes without any prompting from me. He has been able to do everything! — *October 2004*

ANOTHER TEACHER REPORTS:
Just thought I'd give you a heads up on the much more efficient Parent-Teacher Conferences I have had because of your teachings from Lou Tice. I was working with a mom who came into the conference believing that she was a "math dummy" who also had one as a son. She left ready to convince her struggling son that she was the "math genius" to help him, and that they would figure it out together. On a personal note, the simple *21 Keys* techniques that I have already used are making a remarkable difference in my home with my own family. Thank you ever so much! — *October 2004*

A TEACHER WRITES:
After participating in *21 Keys,* I found I had new tools to help my students approach learning in a different way. The first week following my use of the tools, 23 out of 24 test takers earned 100% on their spelling tests – and the other student only missed one word! I noticed that over a 4-6 week period, the spelling scores were rising. Now, the students and I use these tools every week. — *December 2003*

A PARENT WRITES:
I just have to tell you about the experience I had with my son today. He had to give his "Famous Person" presentation this morning in English. He was very nervous and asked me if I thought he could do a good job. Of course, I said, "It's just like you to do a fantastic job. You will speak loudly and clearly." Before I learned about *21 Keys,* I would have said, "Now, don't do this... and make sure not to do that..." This morning it never occurred to me to plant any seed of doubt about whether he would do well or not. Sure enough, he gave the presentation and did a fantastic job just like I knew he would and just like he knew he would. I'm sharing this with you because it is just one more example that *21 Keys* works. — *November 2003*

Based on anecdotal feedback over the past few years, effective implementation of *21 Keys* makes a significant impact on teaching and learning. The teacher that utilizes the concepts gives students the tools to reach their potential. The school that embeds these concepts into the culture moves forward with momentum and focus. The district that builds accountability from top to bottom is more effective at reaching each child and teaching them how to cause their own success. The results of *21 Keys* are seen not just in tangibles such as better achievement scores and retention of good teachers, but also in the all-important intangibles, such as school climate, unity of purpose and commitment to results. The bottom line is, that's what education is all about.

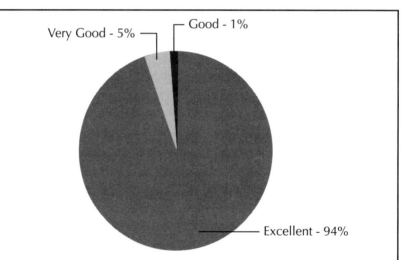

Approximately 4800 school personnel have taken *21 Keys for High Performance Teaching and Learning*™ affecting approximately 140,000 students per year. The above chart reflects the participant evaluations of the program, extrapolated from a random sample group of 426 evaluations. 94% found the course Excellent; 5% Very Good; 1% Good; 0% Fair; and 0% Poor.

Hospital Culture
Noble Goals

By Ken Smithmier, CEO
Decatur Memorial Hospital

I am pleased to participate in a conference whose purpose is to provide information about the helpfulness of The Pacific Institute in our development of an effective culture at the Decatur Memorial Hospital. In my mind, when I think about meetings, they tend to be one of three categories: They tend to be a "why" a "what" or a "how" meeting. I could do a "how" meeting in my sleep. What really interests me the most is the "why."

I can tell you a lot about the things we have done – the whats that we have done and the hows, and I probably will do so. But the bigger issue to me is the "why," particularly when I talk to my colleagues in Illinois and other states about what we have done about this cultural change concept, and the work we have done with The Pacific Institute. It is very easy for me to talk to colleague CEOs, and say these are the steps we are taking and this is how it gets implemented. I shall focus on the steps that were taken, the people who have participated and the things we have learned. I always struggle a little bit when I start to say why we have done it: Why spend the money? Why spend the time? Those are the hard questions, and frequently in my mind I come to the conclusion that the harder the questions, the more time I should spend on figuring it out, because if it's a difficult question, I've got to come to some resolution in my mind before I can really make progress.

I saw Lou at breakfast this morning and I told him that I was going to incorporate three examples to get through this. One, I'm going to talk about the thoroughbred horse racing industry in the United States, because I know that Lou likes horses. Secondly, I want to talk a little bit about an 18th Century Quaker. And thirdly, I would like to talk about Eric Clapton. (This, by the way, is the sort of stuff that drives my wife nuts, and it also probably explains why she has taken a back seat closest to the door, so that if this really blows up, she can just take the exit and sort of *not be with me.)*

Let's talk about horseracing first. I know that many of you are not from the United States, but perhaps whether or not you are from the USA, you know something about the Triple Crown. The Triple Crown is the premier event for American horseracing. It's been held once a year for about 125 years, and it consists of three races. The horse that wins all three races wins the Triple Crown. It starts with the Kentucky Derby at Churchill Downs in Kentucky. It then goes to the Preakness Stakes in Baltimore, Maryland, and then ends at Belmont in New York. The last Triple Crown winner was in 1978.

I kind of got inoculated in 1973, when I was 19 years old, when for some reason I happened to see the running of the Belmont when Secretariat, one of the greatest horses ever, won by something like 23 lengths. He won by such a distance that the other horses weren't even in the range of the camera unless they panned far back of Secretariat.

There was an exciting story this year about a horse named Smarty Jones, who not only was thought to be a candidate to win the Triple Crown, but a horse who added a romantic vein to the story. One of his owners was a pulmonary cripple, an elderly man in a wheelchair.

His jockey was a broken down alcoholic who was known more for his brushes with the law than he was for his success as a jockey. Smarty Jones' trainer was sort of a no-name trainer, and the horse, a Cliff Young type in that everyone in horse training knows that great horses don't come out of Pennsylvania. They come out of Florida or California, not Pennsylvania. Nevertheless, Smarty won the Kentucky Derby, and he won the Preakness by 10 or 11 lengths. He really blew the field away.

The anticipation coming into the Belmont this year was huge. Belmont is known as the Big Sandy, because the soil on the Belmont track is deep and sandy, and if you have ever run on a sandy beach, you know what that's like. Also, the difficult part of the Triple Crown is that the horses run three races in five weeks: one a mile, another a mile and an eighth, and the third, a mile and a quarter. Also the Belmont has big sweeping curves, a big challenge for an inexperienced horse.

There were two horses that were expected to give Smarty tremendous competition. One was Purge and the other was Rock Hard 10. Smarty started off in the ninth position, so he was not in on the fence. He was out a little bit, but he broke from the gate very cleanly and got into the middle of the pack safely. He established himself well. Sure enough, here comes Purge at about the half to the three-quarter mark to challenge him. As Smarty had done in prior races, he just hits this other gear, and Purge was not to be seen again.

At about the mile mark, here comes Rock-Hard 10, considered to be a big threat to Smarty. Smarty hit the gear again, and Rock Hard 10 wilted and just faded from the pack.

My wife and I had a social event that evening which appeared to conflict with the Belmont race. I made it clear that I would either watch the Belmont at our host's home or stay at home for the conclusion of the race, and then go to the social event. (That gives you a picture of how important the Triple Crown was to me.)

After Smarty knocks out Rock Hard 10, he bursts from the pack while I was screaming in my living room, and the 130,000 fans who had been captivated by the allure of Smarty were going crazy. There were no tickets on the ground because people were holding on to them as that was going to be their souvenir of Smarty capturing the 2004 Triple Crown.

And so he broke from the pack, and it just looked like he was going to hit that gear that caused him to win the Preakness by 11 lengths. Then out of nowhere on the outside comes this no-name horse called Birdstone. Little by little, he just sort of reeled Smarty in, and at the line, noses him out. He beats Smarty Jones, knocks out the potential, favored Triple Crown winner, this no-name horse Birdstone.

Now, what does Smarty's jockey, Smarty himself and the Belmont race have to do with competition, achieving, or developing an organizational culture that will result in optimal performance? I started wondering about Smarty's jockey and whether or not he went into the race thinking that he was competing against Purge and Rock Hard 10 or thinking about whether or not he was trying to get the achievement of winning the Triple Crown. And I wonder if, when he defeated Purge and then defeated Rock Hard 10, did perhaps the jockey maybe without consciously thinking about it, relax a little bit? Did he say to himself, "I've got it"? Also, did Smarty feel the jockey relax and Smarty, feeling the jockey relax, think he had it too? And then here comes the competitor and knocks him out.

That's what happens in health care, and that's what happens in a lot of businesses. I think we get consumed with the issue of who we're competing with, and we determine our success by what we've done better than someone else rather than by measuring our success against some high standard, or as we heard in Lou's opening comments yesterday, some noble goal. I fear too often we get wrapped up in that competition, and then misread who the competition is, and a Birdstone equivalent comes out of nowhere and knocks us out. Once you get knocked out, whether it is in life or business, it's a big hole to dig out of.

I will tell you a little about my hospital. We're in Decatur, Illinois, in the middle of the state and the middle of our nation. We are what would be considered a middle to large hospital, 2400 employees, about 300 physicians, 100 of which have been added the last five years, the second largest employer in Decatur. We are approximately the size of Caterpillar. We have the typical services that a hospital has. Additionally we have invested much in Neurosurgery and Oncology, and in Information Technology.

Decatur Memorial Hospital is experiencing success. Over the last five years our market share has gone up, up, up from 56% to 70%. It keeps climbing. Our outpatient activity has gone from 207,000 visits to about 287,000 visits. Our financials are strong. Our community relations are good. Our relationships with our doctors are good. Our bonds are A rated by S&P and Moody's. Our employee relationships are good. So you might look at our hospital and say we are really cruising. The question is, toward what?

The question is, are we competing against someone or something, and are we using data to measure our success against our competitors? Or do we have some kind of noble goal, or goals, to determine whether or not we're really achieving something that matters, regardless of what everybody else is doing?

Laural mentioned some of the difficult issues that we are dealing with. No matter how many difficulties I think I have in the hospital business, I can talk to somebody in another industry and they tell me worse stories than I have. I've never had problems like federal quality mandates, liability insurance and unionization efforts. We've placed a lot of emphasis on improving service and clinical quality.

Yesterday you heard about Caterpillar's efforts with Six Sigma. We launched Six Sigma at our hospital about two and a half years ago with initiatives aimed at people, programs and patients. We've had some success with Six Sigma in things like our emergency department, and our patients' satisfaction with the ER in what is called "door-to-doc" time, meaning the time elapsed from the moment you walk in the door until you are face to face with a physician. Patients tend to feel that the shorter that time is, even if the whole stay is long, at least their care is under way. We've really shortened the door-to-doc time.

We've made tremendous strides in reducing our medication errors and infection rates, particularly with our ICUs. We've also made great strides in reducing waiting times. But all along, within me – and I think within many others at the hospital – there is this desire for more reduction of patients waiting. We know that we are good, but we also know that we are not great.

I bet that our organization is just like yours. We tend to be more acutely aware of our shortcomings than anybody else, and I believe we're more self-critical than most hospitals. We've had some successes but not everywhere. We found some of our successes to have limited sustainability, because we haven't really reached the essence of people. I think this is due to the fact that much of what we've done has not been described in terms of noble goals nor necessarily in terms of overarching achievement.

(For those of you who are considering using Six Sigma, I would say that it is an excellent process. However, Six Sigma alone can be a sterile process. In all of my years of doing this work, I've not found anything from a quality improvement point of view that has the value that Six Sigma has. It is a high-quality, rigid, statistically driven system that we think is terrific, but you have to do more than that.)

Then along come our "who-saids," our friends at Caterpillar in Decatur. You heard Janice Kirby mention Rod Bussell who runs that plant. Rod has had more influence on me than probably he recognizes. I would run into him here and there, and he would talk to me about this Pacific Institute stuff. Initially I would tell people in Decatur that the first time I heard of their programs I thought it was this hold hands and sing Kumbaya sort of stuff, and that's not for me. So I would just sort of politely listen to Rod, but keep him at arm's length.

I finally got to the point, as hardheaded as I can be at times, that when you listen to a guy like Rod, and you see the successes – the quantifiable successes that he's had in his plant – I said to myself, "Okay, if this will work in a heavily unionized, frequently difficult labor-management manufacturing environment, then I ought to pay some attention to this Pacific Institute program to see what we can do with it in the hospital." So we've gone through The Pacific Institute program that most of you have experienced. One thing in particular that we learned was, like Six Sigma, you can't succeed without absolute commitment at the top.

A couple of months ago Lou was in Chicago and he and I did a joint presentation to a senior leadership group of many Illinois hospitals. At the end of the meeting, I extended an open invitation to every hospital in the state of Illinois, inviting them to participate in TPI's *Imagine 21*™ program with our staff, free of charge. Consistent with our belief that commitment from the top was necessary, the attendance of the CEO's of the hospitals was required.

We're now going through the *Leadership Impact Analysis,* the organizational culture consensus building program which tracks progress of an organization in moving away from a less productive defensive culture to a more productive constructive culture. Briefly, in constructive cultures, members, among other traits, are engaged in the organization's development, oriented toward the welfare of the total organization, involved in the development of an organization's vision and goals, and are effective as a member of a team. Briefly, defensive culture members are the antithesis of members of constructive cultures. It is important to note that the system used to distinguish constructive and defensive cultures yields quantitative data derived from the organization's members' responses to a statistically valid questionnaire. From our members' responses to the questionnaire, we have found that the use of both Six Sigma and TPI has worked very well. Both contribute significantly to our development of a constructive culture.

Some of the preliminary results I can give you are what some would say anecdotal or qualitative, not quantitative data: Quantitatively, 80% to 90% of our employees truly have embraced what they have learned in the *Imagine 21*™ curriculum, as revealed by their responses on a reliable and valid questionnaire. Qualitative data, which are sometimes more convincing than information gained through highly controlled experiments, include observations we have made of constructive changes in the attitudes of our managers and our staff, and in some cases, even some of our most negative staff, some of whom were targeted by their supervisors to be the first ones to attend the program.

I was tipped off by our surgery director that she had her most negative employee in a participating group. I attended this group meeting to do a wrap-up on Day Two. Here comes this employee walking up to me. I thought, "Won't this be interesting." She introduced herself to me, told me where she worked and then said, "You know, I watch these units, and that's me. I'm 99% negative, 1% positive, but I'm going to work tomorrow and be a different person. They're not even going to know who I am. They're going to wonder what I'm doing.

They're going to wonder what I've taken." I called her supervisor at home that night, and I said, "Sally, I thought I should alert you to this. I think it's all good news, but you should know what Regina has in her mind tonight."

Then we had a visit about other topics, including a confirmation notice of folks here from an organization in Illinois called a "quality control improvement organization" (QIO). United States Healthcare hospitals have to follow quality standards set by Medicare, and these QIOs oversee that program. Recent guidelines from the QIOs indicate that they want to work with institutions and clinicians who achieve near perfect levels of performance. By the way, in the United States, if all hospitals are 99% accurate in surgeries that we do, we will do 5000 surgeries wrong a week. That's at the 1 Sigma level. So when people talk about being 99% good or being near perfect, you had better pin them down. That's the beauty of Six Sigma, because at 99% if it's you getting cut, that's not enough. Think about that the next time you are admitted to a hospital. Don't tell them I said so.

Here is the bigger piece, though. They want to work with providers to achieve transformational change, and so I say to my colleagues, "If this is what Medicare is telling us to do, how are you going to do it? How are you going to get near-perfect levels of performance?" We surely don't have it now, I guarantee you. I see it from the inside. We surely don't have it now. What are you going to do different for the next 20 years compared to the last 20 years to get transformational rather than incremental change to get those near-perfect levels of performance that is required?

In 1730, there was a Quaker whose name was John Woolman. Quakers at that time were very good at keeping diaries, and Woolman's diaries in particular are considered to be one of the best samples of life in those days. When Woolman was 23 years old, he was working as a clerk. His employer asked him to fill out a bill of sale on a slave.

This was in 1743. Instantly, Woolman was bothered by that. He had cognitive dissonance that said to him, "I am a Quaker and I believe in all the things that Quakers believe, and now I'm going to fill out a piece of paper to process the sale of another human being."

Woolman spent the rest of his life doing what he could to eliminate slavery from all Quaker colonies. He talked with Quakers, one by one, and he talked with Quaker colonies one by one. Woolman died in 1773, and about 20 years after his death, the last vestige of slavery was erased from the last Quaker colony in the United States. Although Woolman didn't do it single-handedly, he is clearly credited with having the largest role in the elimination of slavery from Quaker colonies. And he did it one by one, person by person, organization by organization. He knew what he was trying to achieve, and he wasn't trying to compete with anyone. He wasn't trying to make himself look better than anybody else. He just knew what his goal was, and ultimately he got it done, although regrettably, he didn't live to see the final result.

In a modern-day sense, Eric Clapton has done similar things. I was born in 1954, so my teenage years were in the late 60s and 70s when rock stars were first being deified, and I thought Eric Clapton was the deity to beat all deities. By the way, I saw him in Dallas a few weeks ago. Terri and I were at a meeting in Dallas, sitting at the hotel pool, and here goes Eric Clapton swimming by. I told my wife, "That's Eric Clapton," and she told me that he's not Eric Clapton. I then told her again that it was Eric Clapton, that I know him. He was playing with his two children. I didn't talk to him, since I'm not an autograph-seeker. It surprised me when he walked away from the pool with his two children in a two-person stroller. At that time, I had difficulty understanding what I was seeing – a picture of Eric Clapton without amplifiers and speakers that could blow my eardrums out, pushing a stroller containing his two children.

Both Eric Clapton and John Woolman have worked all their lives avoiding commercial success. That trait is very apparent in Clapton's interviews. For similar reasons, Woolman tried to avoid commercial successes he had during the later years of his life. Both were afraid that such a focus would detract from their main goal in life: for Woolman, to serve God; for Clapton, to not produce music that didn't satisfy him, that would not meet his mission, or wasn't his goal.

I guess that's where I end my comments. I believe that in your business or mine, it's not competing that does it. It is knowing what the goal is not so much in business terms, although, of course we all have to use business metrics to measure our performance. I'm certainly not naive about that, but I think it's more important knowing what the goal is, and knowing how we measure achievement in personal terms for ourselves, our employees, our families, and for whatever social and work situations we may be in. When we get to that point, we really know what the important goals are, and how we can move toward them. I think this is the essence of what The Pacific Institute teaches us.

There may be people who misunderstand The Pacific Institute's mission, but as Lou so correctly pointed out, the lesson will come out over time and it will be shown in actions. And in the end, that will be the most meaningful mission of all.

Bibliography

Aspinwall, L.G. and Staudinger, U. M., (Eds) *A Psychology of Human Strengths.* American Psychological Association, 2003.

Bandura, A. (1994) "Self-Efficacy" *Encyclopedia of Human Behavior,* Volume 4, Academic Press.

Bandura, A. (1989) "Human Agency in Social Cognitive Theory" *American Psychologist.*

Bandura, A. (1986) *Social Foundations of Thought and Action – A Social Cognitive Theory.* Englewood Cliffs, N.J. Prentice Hall.

Cameron, K.S., Dutton, Jane E., and Quinn, R.E. (Eds) *Positive Organizational Scholarship: Foundations of a New Discipline.* Berrett–Koehler Publishers, Inc. San Francisco. 2003.

Cook, R. and Szumal, J., "Measuring Normative Beliefs and Shared Behavioral Expectations: The Reliability and Validity of the Organizational Culture Inventory." *Psychological Reports.* June 1993.

Darce, Keith, Newhouse News Service article in The Seattle Times, 2005

Frederickson, Barbara L., "Positive Emotions and Upward Spirals in Organizations." *Positive Organizational Scholarship.* Cameron et al (Eds) Berrett-Koehler Publishers, San Francisco, 2003.

Hinton, R. *The Cultural Background of Personality.* Appleton Century Crofts. 1945. Page 31.

Jahoda, "The Shifting Sands of Culture" (2002) in Boski, F.J.R. and Van de Vijver and Chodyncka (Eds) *New Directions in Cross-Cultural Psychology. Selected Papers from the 15th International Congress of the International Association of Cross-Cultural Psychology.* Pages 91-106. Warsaw Polish Psychological Association.

Keyes, C. L. M. and Haidt, J. (Eds). Flourishing: *A Positive Psychology and a Life Well Lived.* American Psychological Association, 2002.

Kotter, J.P., and Heskett, J.H., *Corporate Culture and Performance.* The Free Press. New York, 1992.

Kroebor, A.L. and Kluckhohn, C. (1952) "Culture: A Critical Review of Concepts and Definitions." Peabody Museum of Archeology and Ethnology. Cambridge, MA Volume 47, No. 1.

Lopez, J. and Snyder, C.R., (Eds) *Positive Psychological Assessment – A Handbook of Models and Measures.* 2003.

Mead, M,. *Coming of Age in Samoa.* William Morrow and Company (1930); Quill (1973); and HarperCollins (2001).

Peterson, C. and Seligman, M. (Eds) *Character Strengths and Virtues: A Handbook and Classification.* APA and Oxford University Press.

Smith, D. *"Albert Bandura's Social Cognitive Theory is the foundation of television and radio shows that have changed the lives of millions."* "The Theory Heard 'Round the World." Monitor on Psychology (2002).

Spreitzer, G.M. and Sonenshein, S., "Positive Deviance and Extraordinary Organizations." *Positive Organizational Scholarship.* Cameron et al (Eds) Berrett-Koehler Publishers, San Francisco, 2003.

Sternberg, R. J. and Grigorenko, E. L. (Eds) *Culture and Competence: Contexts of Life Success,* American Psychological Association, 2004.

Sutcliff, K.M. and Vogus, T.J., "Organizing for Resilience" *Positive Organizational Scholarship.* Cameron et al (Eds) Berrett-Koehler Publishers, San Francisco, 2003.

Tice, L., "Leadership and Changing Cultures" *European CEO,* January-February 2005, Pages 66-67.

Van Schaik, Carel, et al, "Orangutan Cultures and the Evolution of Material Culture" *Science,* 3 January, Volume 299, Pages 102- 105.

Vaughn, D. *The Columbia Decision: Risky Technology, Culture and Deviance at NASA.* University of Chicago Press, 1996.